The Secret of Gold

How to Get What You Want

Robert Collier

All rights reserved. No part of this publication may be reproduced, stored in a retrieval system, or transmitted in any form or by any means, electronic, mechanical, photocopying or otherwise, without the prior permission of the copyright owner.

For information regarding special discounts for bulk purchases, please contact BN Publishing at info@bnpublishing.com

©Copyright 2007 – BN Publishing

www.bnpublishing.com

ALL RIGHTS RESERVED

Printed in the U.S.A.

CONTENTS

FOREWORD: The Riddle of the Sphinx 6

Chapter 1: The Genii of the Lamp 8

Chapter 2: The Spirit Within 13

Chapter 3: The Lode Star 28

Chapter 4: The Man of Brass 49

Chapter 5: Start Something! 60

Chapter 6: Rough Diamonds 73

Chapter 7: Ich Dien—I Serve 84

Chapter 8: The Coming of the Spirit 92

FOREWORD: The Riddle of the Sphinx

"WHAT is it," asked the Sphinx, "that walks on four legs in the morning, on two legs at noon and on three legs in the evening?" And all who passed her way had to answer that question—*or be devoured!*

That was the Riddle of the Sphinx of olden days. But to modern man has come a far more difficult one—

"How can I earn more money? How can I make enough to get the necessities and the comforts of life to which my family and I are entitled?"

That is the eternal question which confronts you and will haunt you every day until you solve it. That is the present-day Riddle of the Sphinx that devours all who fail to answer it.

For lack is the greatest evil that mankind has to contend with.

Yet every man knows that in this old earth of ours are riches and abundance sufficient not merely for every soul now on this planet—but for all who ever will be! And in the very first chapter of the Bible, It is written that, "God gave man dominion over all the earth."

Not only that, but more than half the prophecies in the Scriptures refer to the time when man shall possess the earth. When tears and sorrow shall be unknown. When riches and abundance shall be yours for the taking.

That time is here—here and now for those who understand the power and the availability of that mysterious, half recognized Spirit within which so few people know, but which, fully understood, can do anything.

But in no book ever written is there any complete explanation of this Spirit within, any complete directions for availing one's-self of its infinite power and understanding. In no book, that is, but one!

And in the following pages I shall show you what that one Book is and

FOREWORD: The Riddle of the Sphinx

where to find the directions which tell you how to harness this truly illimitable power, how to make it bring to you anything of good you may desire. For—

"There hath not failed one word of all His good promises, which He promised by the hand of Moses, His servant."—I. KINGS, 8:56.

— ROBERT COLLIER

Chapter 1: The Genii of the Lamp

"Thou gavest also Thy Good Spirit to instruct them, and withheldest not thy manna from their mouth, and gavest them water for their thirst."—NEHEMIAH 9:20.

IN AN ancient town in far off Cathay, there once lived a poor young man named Aladdin. His father had been a tailor, but died before he could teach his profession to his son, and the boy and his widowed mother were frequently hard put to get enough to eat.

But despite his poverty, Aladdin was one of those cheerful souls who find life good. Many and often were the times that found him wandering joyfully in the mountains, when he should have been seeking the elusive yen in some odd job among his neighbors. And Fortune, looking down upon his cheery hopefulness, smiled—as has been the habit of Fortune since time began—for then, as now, she was a fickle jade, loving most those who worry least about her.

One day, wandering among the hills, Aladdin discovered a cave, its entrance closed by a great stone. Prying the stone away, he entered, and found therein a lamp burning upon a shelf. Thinking to use it at home, Aladdin stuck the lamp in his belt and, departing, took it with him.

Next morning, lacking the wherewithal for breakfast, he bethought him of this lamp, and since it looked old and tarnished, started to polish it in the hope of thus bringing for it a better price. What was his astonishment and terror to see immediately appear before him a Genii of gigantic proportions, who, however, made humble obeisance: "I am the slave of the lamp," quoth he, "ready to do the bidding of him who holds the lamp. What would you of me?"

Terrified though he was, Aladdin could understand that. So he took heart of grace, and decided to see if this great Genii really was as

Chapter 1: The Genii of the Lamp

good as his word. "I am hungry," he therefore told him. "Bring me something to eat." The Genii disappeared. An instant later he was back again with a sumptuous repast!

Aladdin ate and was satisfied. And when next he hungered, summoned the Genii and ate again. Thereafter, to one so used to hunger, life was one grand song—just one endless succession of eating and sleeping, sleeping and eating again.

Until one day the Sultan's daughter passed that way. Her eyes had the mischievous sparkle in their depths that has drawn hermits from their cells. Her lips were twin rubies. Her teeth pearls.

So much Aladdin saw—and was enchanted. Life took on a new meaning. There was more to it than eating and sleeping after all. Here was something to live for, work for, hope for. Even though at the moment it never occurred to him that he might ever hope to win such loveliness, such divinity, for himself.

But then he bethought him of his Genii. If the Genii could bring him food, raiment, riches—why not position and power, too? Why not the Sultan's daughter? Why not, in fact, the Sultan's place? He decided to try.

First he astonished the Sultan with the magnificence of the gifts with which his good Genii furnished him. Then he built a palace more beautiful far than that of the Sultan himself. Finally he presented himself as suitor for the hand of the beautiful princess.

The Sultan laughed at the idea. But one cannot continue to laugh at a man whose raiment is more costly, whose retinue more splendid, whose palace more magnificent than one's own. One can only vie with him in splendour, and failing that—either fight him or take him into one's own camp.

The Sultan tried to vie with him. But princely riches could not

Chapter 1: The Genii of the Lamp

compare with those of the Genii. He tried fighting. But who could hope to cope with the powers of the invisible world?

At last he decided to share that wealth, to benefit by that power. And so it came about that Aladdin won the lovely Princess of his dreams.

Fairy tales—you will say. And of course, they are. But back of them is more than mere childish fable. There is the Wisdom and the Mysticism of the East—so frequently hidden in parable or fable.

For those Wise Men of the East had grasped, thousands of years ago, the fundamental fact—so hard for our Western minds to realize—that deep down within ourselves, far under our outer layers of consciousness, is a Power that far transcends the power of any conscious mind.

"The Holy Spirit within us," deeply religious people term it. And, truly, its power is little short of Divine.

"Our Subconscious Mind," so the Scientists call it.
Call it what you will, it is there—all unknown to most of us—a sleeping Giant who, aroused, can carry us on to fame and fortune overnight; A Genii-of-the-Brain more powerful, more the servant of our every right wish, than was ever Aladdin's fabled Genii-of-the-Lamp of old.

Health and happiness, power and riches, lie ready to its hand. You have but to wake it, to command it, to get of it what you will. It is part of you—yet its power is limitless. It is Mind—Thought—Idea. It is an all-powerful mental magnet that can draw to you anything you may desire.

Just as electricity turns the inert electric bulb into a thing of light and life—just as the gasoline vapor turns your motor into a creature of speed and action—just as steam awakens the locomotive into an

Chapter 1: The Genii of the Lamp

engine of power and usefulness—so this mental magnet can vitalize YOU into a Being capable of accomplishing ANY TASK YOU MAY SET, capable of rising to any height, capable of winning love, honor and riches.

You have seen hypnotists put subjects to sleep. You have seen men and women, while in this hypnotic trance, do marvelous feats of mind reading or of mental arithmetic. You have seen others show wonderful endurance or physical strength.

I remember one hypnotist who, after putting his subject in a trance, would assure him that he (the subject) was a bar of iron. Then the hypnotist would stretch him out between two chairs—his head on one, his feet on another—and pile weights upon him, or have several people stand upon him. A feat of strength that the subject could never have accomplished in his ordinary mind. Yet did it without strain or difficulty under the influence of the hypnotist.

How did he do it? Simply by removing the control of the conscious mind—by putting it to sleep—and leaving the Subconscious in sole charge. The power is in your body to do anything—only your conscious mind doesn't believe that it is. Remove these conscious inhibitions—place the Subconscious in entire charge—and there is nothing beyond your capacity to perform.

The hypnotist does his tricks by putting your conscious mind to sleep and then suggesting to your Subconscious the things he wants it to do. But it is in no wise necessary to deal with the Subconscious through some third party. It is no part of the Divine plan that you must first put yourself under some outside control. On the contrary, those who learn to use their own Subconscious Minds can accomplish far greater wonders with their bodies, with their brains, with their fortunes than could any hypnotist for them.

It is to show you how to properly use this Genii-of-your-Mind, how to summon it, how to control it, that this Course is written.

Chapter 1: The Genii of the Lamp

"But where shall wisdom be found? And where is the place of understanding?"—JOB 28:12.

"There is a Spirit in man; and the inspiration of the Almighty giveth him understanding."—JOB 32:8.

Chapter 2: The Spirit Within

YOU often hear a man spoken of as brainy. The idea being that he has more gray matter in his cranium than most of us. And for years the size of a man's head or the shape of his "bumps" was believed to indicate his mentality.

But science now shows that one man has just as good brains as another. Differences in weight or shape or size have nothing to do with it. Each of us has a perfect brain to start with. It is what we put *into* it and the way we *use* it that counts—not the size or weight!

Brains are merely the storehouse of the mind. They are not the mind itself. Each individual brain cell—and there are some nine billions of them—is like a phonograph record on which impressions are registered through the thousands of nerves from all over the body that center in the brain.

Once registered, that impression stays as long as the brain cell remains. When we have no occasion to use an impression for a long time, it is filed away in the nine-billion filing compartment—and apparently forgotten.

But it is never really forgotten. It can always be recalled by the proper suggestion to the subconscious mind. The only thing that can permanently destroy the impression is the removal of the brain cell itself. That is why injuries to the brain so frequently result in complete loss of memory as to many events in the individual's life.

But the registering of impressions is merely the first step. The animals have that. The next—and the step that puts man so far above all other creatures—is the reasoning mind. Mind uses the brain cells to recall any impression it may need. To compare them. To draw conclusions from them. In short, to reason!

Chapter 2: The Spirit Within

That is the most important province of mind. But it has another—the regulating, governing and directing of the growth and functions of the body. So complicated an affair that no conscious mind in the universe could ever grope with it.

Yet the subconscious mind does it with ease—does it for the youngest infant as well as for you or me—in fact, frequently does it better.

From the earliest moment of our birth, the subconscious mind takes control. It directs the beating of the heart, the breathing of the lungs, the complicated processes of digestion and assimilation. And the less it is interfered with, the better work it does.

Your body is the most wonderful and complicated chemical factory in the world. Made up of water, coal, iron, lime, sugar, phosphorus, salt, hydrogen and iodine, no man living could figure out the changes made necessary in its composition from minute to minute by heat, by cold, by pressure from without or by food taken within. No chemist in all the world could tell you how much water you should drink to neutralize the excess salt in salt fish. How much you lose through perspiration. How much water, how much salt, how much of each different element in your food should be absorbed into your blood each day to maintain perfect health.

Yet your subconscious mind knows. Knows without effort. Knows even when you are an infant. And furthermore, acts immediately upon that knowledge.

To quote the Rev. Wm. T. Walsh—"The subconscious mind directs all the vital processes of our body. You do not think consciously about breathing. Every time you take a breath you do not have to reason, decide, command. The SUBCONSCIOUS MIND sees to that. You have not been at all conscious that you have been breathing while you have been reading this page. So it is with the mind and the circulation of blood. The heart is a muscle like the

Chapter 2: The Spirit Within

muscle of your arm. It has no power to move itself or to direct its action. Only mind, only something that can think, can direct our muscles, including the heart. You are not conscious that you are commanding your heart to beat. The subconscious mind attends to that. And so it is with the assimilation of food, the building and repairing of the body. In fact, all the vital processes are looked after by the subconscious mind."

Whence comes all this wonderful knowledge? Whence comes the intelligence that enables day-old infants to figure out problems in chemistry that would confound the most learned professors? Whence but from the same Mind that regulates the planets in their courses, that puts into the acorn the image of the mighty oak it is to be, and then shows it how to draw from the sunlight, from the air, from the earth, from the water, the nutriment necessary to build that image into reality.

That Mind is God. And the subconscious in us is our part of Divinity. It is the Holy Spirit within.

The Bible teaches one Universal God, Father of all things, *the life of all things animate.*
And modern science shows us that all things are animate—even the rocks and the dirt beneath our feet. Even the supposedly dead piece of paper on which these words are printed. All are made up of tiny particles called atoms. And the atoms in turn consist of protons and electrons—bits of electrical energy, so minute as to be invisible to the naked eye, but very much alive and constantly moving, constantly changing.

In *The Secret of the Ages,* the consistency of matter is explained in detail. For those who have not read this explanation, suffice it here to quote from the *New York Herald-Tribune:*

"We used to believe that the universe was composed of an unknown number of different kinds of matter, one kind for each

Chapter 2: The Spirit Within

chemical element. The discovery of a new element had all the interest of the unexpected. It might turn out to be anything, to have any imaginable set of properties.

"That romantic prospect no longer exists. We know now that instead of many ultimate kinds of matter there are only two kinds. Both of these are really kinds of electricity. One is negative electricity, being, in fact, the tiny particle called the electron, familiar to radio fans as one of the particles vast swarms of which operate radio vacuum tubes. The other kind of electricity is positive electricity. Its ultimate particles are called protons. From these protons and electrons all of the chemical elements are built up. Iron and lead and oxygen and gold and all the others differ from one another merely in the number and arrangement of the electrons and protons which they contain. That is the modern idea of the nature of matter. *Matter is really nothing but electricity.*"

Everything has life in it. And life is God, Therefore, everything in this world, everything in the heavens above, in the earth beneath, or in the waters under the earth, is a manifestation of God.

God is life. He is the life in us. And the life in all created things. He is the "Father" in you. He is the life-force, the God-force, that flows through every atom of your being. Make yourself one with Him, and there is nothing you cannot do.

A great religious teacher once said that there are just two things in the Universe—God and His manifestations. Really there is just one —for God is in all His manifestations.

One of the Bible's greatest teachings is that ALL MEN ARE EQUALLY THE CHILDREN OF GOD!

Just think—if God is the Father of ALL men, then ALL are His children, equally entitled to the good things of life, equally dear to Him! This is the greatest message ever brought to any planet! That

Chapter 2: The Spirit Within

man is the son of God. That he inherits from the Father all of life, all of wisdom, all of riches, all of power.

God is the Parent. And man's every quality is derived from Him. Not only that, but *man inherits every quality of the Father!* He has only to grow up in knowledge, to learn the Father's ways, to lean trustfully upon the Father's help, in order to be supreme "amid the war of elements, the wreck of matter and the crush of worlds."

Apart from God, man is a weakling, the sport of circumstances, the victim of any force strong enough to overpower or brush him aside.

But let him ally himself with the Father, and he becomes, instead of the creature of law, the ruler through law. Instead of the sport of circumstance, he makes circumstances. Instead of the victim of fire or water or sickness or poverty, he masters the forces of nature, demands health and prosperity as his birthright.

The God that most of us were taught to believe in was a huge patriarchal Man-God, seated upon a throne high up in the skies. A King—stern, righteous and just— chastening His children mercilessly whenever He felt it was for their good. Holding an exact scale between the good they had done and the sins they had committed. And dispensing penances or rewards to balance the two.

Today, we are coming around to the idea of a loving Father-God. A God that is in each one of us, whose "good pleasure it is to give us the Kingdom", and to promise these same powers to us!

How, then, shall we take advantage of our son-ship? How use the infinite power it puts in our hands?

The purpose of this book is to develop the divinity that is in you. What is the first thing to do? Where shall you start? What shall you do?

Chapter 2: The Spirit Within

Reaching Into Infinity

The first essential is to find a point of contact with the Father. Benjamin Franklin sent a kite up into the clouds and brought down along its string a current of electricity. Through him, man has learned to harness this electricity for his daily servant. Franklin made his contact with the source of power.

Thousands of years before Franklin—centuries even before the common era—men began to send up kites (figuratively speaking) trying to contact with the source of life itself.

A few succeeded. A few great Prophets like Elisha, Elijah, Moses, contacted with the Source of all Power, and whenever and as long as they kept that contact, nothing could withstand them.

Franklin caught the source of electrical power, and by learning to understand and work with it, turned those terror-inspiring thunderbolts of destruction into man's greatest friend and servant. The electricity did not change. It is exactly the same now as afore time. It is merely man's conception of it that has changed.

Uncontrolled, lightning was a curse to mankind. Through understanding, man has harnessed it to serve his needs. Touch a button—and it lights your home. Touch another—and it brings to you news and instruction, entertainment and music from hundreds or thousands of miles away. The mere throwing of a switch releases the power of millions of horses. Pulling it out bridles them again. Was ever such a master servant?

Yet it is as nothing to the power latent in the Source of Life—the power of the Father of all things.

Even now, ignorant of this Power as most of us are, we occasionally contact with it, but we do it accidentally—*and we fail*

Chapter 2: The Spirit Within

to maintain the contact.

You know how often inspirational things have "come to you"—snatches of song, or speech, or verse such as man never wrote before. Visions of wonderful achievement. Echoes of great ideas. Glimpses of riches you could almost reach—the riches of the Spirit within.

If only you could tap that boundless Reservoir at will, what success would not be yours, how puny your present accomplishments would seem by comparison!

And you *can* tap it. You can make your contact with Infinity—if not at will—at least with frequency. All that is necessary is understanding and belief.

How to do it? How to go about it? Through the Holy Spirit within you. Through your part of Divinity. Through an understanding of what is commonly known as your Subconscious Mind.

We stumble upon His vast power occasionally—and call our resultant deeds superhuman! We contact now and then with Infinity—and regard the result as a miracle!

There is no such thing as a miracle. The occasional wonder-works that we do—the sudden healing from sickness, the miraculous escape, the answered prayer—are all divinely natural. The miracle is that it happens so seldom. We should be able to establish and keep that contact always! We should be able to contact with and use the power of the Spirit as readily as we now can use the power of electricity.

But just as Franklin had first to determine what the power was that made the lightning, so have you first to learn what is this Holy Spirit within you.

Chapter 2: The Spirit Within

To say that it is the subconscious mind is not enough. It is far more than that. The subconscious mind can be used either for good or for evil. Uncontrolled, it is as great a destructive force as the lightning. If you have read *The Secret of the Ages,* you know that you can suggest thoughts of health or of disease to your subconscious mind, of success or of failure—and whichever image you get across to the subconscious, it will proceed to work out. But the Holy Spirit can be used only for good.

What then is the Holy Spirit?

How do you acquire it? How contact with it?

Have you ever read any of the accounts you occasionally see of people who have been very sick—who have hovered for minutes or for hours right over the Valley of Death—and then come back? Remember their description of how they seemed to be looking down upon themselves, upon the whole scene, as one apart, as one having but a casual interest in what was going on? Remember how some little thing called them back and how frequently they went back with reluctance?

Stewart Edward White had a story in the May *American Magazine* that exactly illustrated the idea. It told of a man who, according to all scientific tests, had died— lay dead, in fact, for two hours. And here, in part, was his description of the experience:

"I was pretty ill before I died, and things about me got somewhat vague and unreal. I suppose I was half dozing, and partly delirious perhaps. I'd slip in and out of focus, as it were. Sometimes I'd see myself and the bed and the room and the people clearly enough; then again I'd sort of drop into an inner reverie inside myself. Not asleep exactly, nor yet awake. You'll get much the same thing sitting in front of a warm fire after a hearty dinner.

"Now, here's a funny one. I don't know if you'll get this: You know

Chapter 2: The Spirit Within

these pictures sent by radio? They are all made up of a lot of separate dots, you know. If you enlarged the thing enough, you'd almost lose the picture, wouldn't you? And you'd have a collection of dots with a lot of space between them. Well, that's how I seemed to myself.

"I could contract myself, bring all the dots close together, and there I'd be, solid as a brick church, lying in bed; and I could expand myself until the dots got separated so far that there were mostly spaces between them. And when I did that my body in the bed got very vague to me, because the dots were so far apart they didn't make a picture; and I—the consciousness of me—was somehow the thing in the spaces that held the dots together at all. I found it quite amusing contracting and expanding like that.

"Then I began to think about it. I began to wonder whether I held the dots together, or whether the dots held me together; and I got so interested that I thought I'd try to find out. You see, I wasn't the dots: I—the essence of me, the consciousness of me—was the spaces between the dots, holding them together. I thought to myself, 'I wonder if I can get away from these dots?' So I tried it; and I could. I must say I was a little scared. That body made of dots was a good, solid container. When I left its shelter, it occurred to me that I might evaporate into universal substance, like letting a gas out of a bottle. I didn't; but I certainly was worried for fear I'd burst out somewhere. I felt awfully thin-skinned!"

Remember how you have sometimes had similar experiences in dreams, when you seemed to be a disembodied spirit looking down on yourself from above?

That disembodied self is the soul of you—your subconscious mind. But it is something more, too. Imbue it with understanding of your oneness with the Father, confirm it with a realization of the God-life flowing so abundantly through you—and it becomes, in addition, *the Holy Spirit within you*—one with the Father, one with

Chapter 2: The Spirit Within

the Source of Life, of Power, of Abundance. In short, the Holy Spirit within you is your subconscious mind, vitalized through direct contact with the Father.

You have been told time and again how small a part of your real abilities you use when you confine your mental work to your conscious mind. Prof. Wm. James, the world-famous Psychologist, estimated that the average man used only 10 percent of his real abilities, while Dr. Mayo compares the mind to an iceberg—one-fourth above water (the conscious mind), and three-fourths submerged (the subconscious). Think, then, if the use of your subconscious mind adds so much to your abilities, how much your value will be increased if you add to that the infinite power of the Holy Spirit!

As the ordinary man uses it, the subconscious mind is largely a bundle of habits. You practice on the piano merely to set up a certain train of actions and reactions so that, after a time, your subconscious can take over the work from your conscious mind. The skilled pianist can play from memory the most difficult pieces and at the same time carry on a spirited conversation. Why? Because two entirely different provinces of the mind are carrying on their functions—the one through the fingers, the other through speech and hearing.

The same thing applies to every physical avocation. To become really skillful at anything, you must get it into the charge of your subconscious mind. As long as your conscious mind must take active control, you are tense, doubtful, hesitant—you blunder, become excited, fail. Let the action become automatic, however—in other words, let your subconscious have charge of it—and you relax naturally and do whatever is required of you without effort and will.

A man's responsiveness to subconscious reactions is usually the measure of his luck or ill luck in avoiding accidents. In the *New*

Chapter 2: The Spirit Within

York Herald-Tribune there was an editorial recently along this very line entitled—"Whom Ill Luck Pursues":

"The Industrial Fatigue Research Board has made an interesting report on the reasons for industrial accidents. It is already well known to thoughtful managers of factories that some men are persistently unlucky. If any one is to suffer a broken leg, it will be one of these individuals. When minor accidents are being dealt out by Fate these unfortunates never fail to receive more than their reasonable shares. No definite fault can be found with them. They are not noticeably careless or foolhardy. The poor things seem simply to possess an incurable propensity for being at hand when anything happens. Like the conventional innocent bystander, they are, almost by definition, the persons who get hurt.

"Armed with the modern magician's wand of careful record and exact statistical inquiry, two investigators for the research board have traced these instances of persistent ill luck to their cause. No demon of bad luck is concerned, although the uninstructed may well think so when they read that the cause's name is aesthetakinetic co-ordination. Translated into English, this means a lack of that instinct and exact correspondence between warning and action which some people possess and some do not. If a board in the floor is loose and happens to fly up when stepped on, some people will jump instantly and in the right direction. Others will move the wrong way or not at all. If a chair breaks some sitters will land on their feet, others on the floor. Under the conditions of modern civilization it is usually the latter who are being taken to the hospital."

The functions of your body—your heart, lungs, stomach, liver, the continual breaking down and rebuilding of all the cells—these, too, are the province of your subconscious mind. And as long as they are left to it in the full assurance that it knows its work and is tending faithfully to it, all will be well with them.

Chapter 2: The Spirit Within

But let the conscious mind interfere, and as in playing the piano or doing any other difficult stunt, trouble will ensue.

Have you ever seen a football team whose classmates did nothing but "knock" it, tell it how rotten it was individually and collectively, how little chance it had of ever winning a game? You know how little chance that team would have of getting even a single goal.

But take that same team, put a real class spirit behind it, surround it with boosters and urge it on with a stirring college yell—and then watch it go!

So it is with your subconscious mind and your body. It knows perfectly how to rebuild your body—how to keep it well. But if you tell it, in effect, that you have no confidence in its ability to do this —if you are continually trying to take over the control through your doubts and fears and worries—you will soon have a mutinous or discouraged crew on your hands, that no longer believes in you or itself. And the result will be nervousness, apathy, failure.

As the Rev. W. John Murray put it— "Whatever order we issue to the subconscious mind, it promptly undertakes to carry out. Whatever state of existence you declare to be in being, the subconscious mind assumes exists and works within you accordingly. If a friend asks you: How do you feel today? And you reply: I am not well; I have a headache; I am all in; I don't feel up to the mark at all, you are unconsciously setting the subconscious mind to work to realize the state you declare yourself to be in. On the other hand if you say: I am well, happy and strong, the subconscious mind undertakes to realize this state for you.

"Hence you can see what a wonderful power is within your control for your happiness or unhappiness, your condition of body and mind, and how necessary it is for you to use this power always in a positive direction. *You are, in a word, what you think you are.* This

Chapter 2: The Spirit Within

is not a theory, a fancy or a fad. It is a law. And the reason why the world is filled with sin, disease, misery and misfortune is because it requires effort to think positive thoughts, while negative thinking is the result of inertia."

But it is not only in running the body-machine that the subconscious shows the power of the Spirit that is behind it. It has all knowledge of outside things as well. Contact with it, and you can learn what you will.

Some time ago there was an article in *The American* telling of the experiences of a convict, formerly the editor of a large newspaper.

Morphine had brought this man to prison. He had started taking it when, as a newspaper man, his body would be so worn out that he could no longer write. By "doping" the conscious mind into unconsciousness, he would bring the subconscious to the fore, with the result that the most wonderful articles flowed from his pen. In one case, without a clue to guide him, he traced a gang of criminals who were in hiding!

But his was not merely an impossible way to contact with the Holy Spirit—it was the wrong way to contact with the subconscious as well—and he paid a fearful price for it.

Take Theodore Roosevelt, on the other hand. When he entered Harvard in 1876, he was thin of chest, be-spectacled, nervous, weighing only 90 pounds. He was afraid to get on his feet and try to make a speech. Compare that with the man he became—the wonder of the world for efficiency, endurance, working power, and joyousness in life. He was a cowboy, a soldier, a lawyer, a statesman, a writer. And he did each of these things phenomenally well.

That is one example of what the right attitude towards the subconscious will do. Then there are those frequent cases you hear about like the one described in *Psychology Magazine*. Henry A.

Chapter 2: The Spirit Within

Wight never studied art—never knew he had any talent for painting. He went into the matter-of-fact-business of steel and coal, and was successful in it. Then when he was getting along in the thirties, he found himself with the desire to paint. So, to use his own laconic explanation, "he did it—that's all." And his monotypes have won the praise of the best critics.

I know a famous songwriter who never studied a note. Her music "just comes to her." I know a man—a successful businessman of nearly fifty—who suddenly started writing poems. Wonderful poems—that have been eagerly accepted by the best magazines. And he doesn't know a rule of prosedy! I know an eminent geologist who never consciously examines a stone. He just walks over his ground abstractedly and then tells—for a very high fee—what is underneath it.

Contacting with the Subconscious—contacting haphazardly, accidentally—yet getting marvelous results while the contact holds!

Whatever you want to know, whatever you wish to do—the knowledge and the power are there.

Ordinary contact with the subconscious is comparatively easy. The first essential is relaxation. To find a really comfortable easy chair or lounge or bed, where one can be quiet, undisturbed, unconscious of oneself and one's surroundings. To stretch luxuriously and then let every muscle relax. To review before your mind's eye every phase of the problem or the subject—not worriedly, not striving for the answer—but merely laying them before the spirit within in the way you would put them before some all-wise Solomon. To *know* that he *has* the answer—and will presently give it to you. To relax thankfully in this knowledge into slumber, with the contented feeling that you have got what you wanted. Do that—and your answer will come.

Chapter 2: The Spirit Within

Dr. W. Hanna Thomson, in "Brain and Personality," gives some instances of how this sometimes works out even when the person doing it has no knowledge of how to put his problem up to his subconscious mind. The first was told him by a fellow student at college. One night his roommate sat up late working at a difficult problem in mathematics. Failing to solve it, he rubbed his slate clean, put out the light and went to bed.

Later on that night the first student was awakened by the light shining in his eyes. Looking up, he saw his friend working away at his slate. The next morning he commented on it, only to have his roommate indignantly deny that he had been up at all during the night. To prove his assertion, the first student got the slate, and there on it was the problem that had puzzled his friend—*all worked out to the correct conclusion!*

The other case Thomson tells of was that of a British Consul in Syria. He had been studying Arabic diligently in an effort to better fit himself for his position, and one night tried to compose a letter to the Emir at Lebanon. After a couple of hours of fruitless effort, he finally lost all patience with the language and the job, and went to bed.

What was his astonishment to find on his desk in the morning a freshly written letter, in his own handwriting, couched in the purest Arabic, that the Slave-of-the-Lamp himself could not have improved upon!
The subconscious mind is your Slave of the Lamp. Use him, in the ways outlined above—and there is no problem he cannot work out for you.

But recognize your relation with God, your oneness with the Source of all life and Power—in short, contact with the Source of Power—and that subconscious mind becomes the Holy Spirit within you, to whom nothing is impossible!

Chapter 3: The Lode Star

THERE once lived in a town of Persia two brothers, one named Cassim, the other Ali Baba. Cassim had married a very rich wife, and become a wealthy but miserly and greedy money-lender. Ali Baba had married a woman as poor as himself, and lived by cutting wood, and bringing it upon his donkeys into the town to sell. But he had married for love and he worked cheerily, asking only of Allah that He watch over his little family and help him to teach his son to tread in the right path.

One day, when Ali Baba was in the forest cutting wood, he saw a great cloud of dust coming towards him from the distance. Observing it attentively, he soon distinguished a body of horsemen, and as honest people had little business that far from the haunts of men he suspected they might be robbers. Greatly frightened, he determined to leave his donkeys and save himself. Yet he was not so frightened as to lose all curiosity, so he climbed up a tree that grew on a high rock, whose branches, while thick enough to conceal him, yet enabled him to see all that passed beneath.

The troop, which numbered about forty, all well mounted and armed, came to the foot of the rock and dismounted. Each man unbridled his horse, tied him to some shrub, and hung about the animal's neck a bag of corn. Then each took off his saddle-bag, which from its weight seemed to Ali Baba to be full of gold and silver. One, whom he took to be their captain, came under the tree in which Ali Baba was concealed; and, making his way through some shrubs, pronounced these words—"Open, Sesame!" The moment the captain of the robbers had thus spoken, a door opened in the rock; and after he had made all his troop enter before him, he followed them, when the door shut again of itself.

The robbers stayed some time within the rock, during which Ali Baba, fearful of being caught, remained in the tree.

Chapter 3: The Lode Star

At last the door opened again, and as the captain went in last, so he came out first, and stood to see them all pass by him. Then Ali Baba heard him make the door close by pronouncing these words, "Shut, Sesame!" The robbers forthwith bridled their horses, and mounted, and when the captain saw them all ready, he put himself at their head, and they returned the way they had come.

Ali Baba followed them with his eyes as far as he could see, and afterward stayed a considerable time before he descended. Remembering the words the captain of the robbers had used to cause the door to open he was curious to see if his pronouncing them would have the same effect. Accordingly, he went among the shrubs, stood before it, and said, "Open, Sesame!" Instantly the door flew wide open.

Ali Baba, who expected a dark, dismal cavern, was surprised to see a well-lighted and spacious chamber, receiving its light from an opening at the top of the rock. Scattered around in profusion were all sorts of rich bales of silk stuff, brocade, and valuable carpeting, gold and silver ingots in great heaps, and money in bags The cave must have been occupied for ages by robbers, one succeeding another.

Ali Baba fell on his knees and thanked Allah, the Most High. "Here," thought he, "is the provision I have prayed for to keep us in our old age and to provide our son with a start in life."
So he went boldly into the cave, and collected as much of the gold coin, which was in bags, as he thought his three donkeys could carry. When he had loaded them with the bags, he laid wood over them in such a manner that they could not be seen. After he had passed in and out as often as he wished, he stood before the door, and pronounced the words, "Shut, Sesame!" and the door closed of itself.

Chapter 3: The Lode Star

When Ali Baba got home, he drove his asses into a little yard, shut the gates very carefully, threw off the wood that covered the panniers, carried the bags into the house, and ranged them in order before his wife. He emptied the bags before his astonished wife, raising such a great heap of gold as to dazzle her eyes. Then he told her the whole adventure from beginning to end, and, above all, recommended her to keep it secret.

The wife rejoiced greatly at their good-fortune, but woman-like, wanted to count the gold piece by piece. "Wife," replied Ali Baba, "never try to number the gifts of Allah. Take them—and be thankful. To number them is to limit them. As for this treasure, I will dig a hole and bury it. There is no time to be lost." "You are in the right, husband," replied she.

"But," she thought, as he departed into the garden with his spade, "it will do no harm to know, as nigh as possible, how much we have. I will borrow a small measure, and measure it."

Away she ran to her brother-in-law Cassim, who lived hard by, and begged his wife for the loan of a measure for a little while. Her sister-in-law asked her whether she would have a great or a small one. The other asked for a small one. She bade her stay a little, and she would readily fetch one.

The sister-in-law did so, but as she knew Ali Baba's poverty, she was curious to know what sort of grain his wife wanted to measure, and, artfully putting some suet at the bottom of the measure, brought it to her, with the excuse that she was sorry that she had made her stay so long, but that she could not find it sooner.

Ali Baba's wife went home, filled the measure with gold and emptied it in the corner. Again and again she repeated that, and when she had done, she was very well satisfied to find the number of measures amounted to so many as they did, and went to tell her husband, who had almost finished digging the hole. While Ali Baba

Chapter 3: The Lode Star

was burying the gold, his wife, to show her exactness and diligence to her sister-in-law, carried the measure back again, but without taking notice that a piece of gold had stuck to the bottom. "Sister," said she, giving it to her again, "you see that I have not kept your measure long. I am obliged to you for it, and return it with thanks."

As soon as Ali Baba's wife was gone, Cassim's wife looked at the bottom of the measure, and was in inexpressible surprise to find a piece of gold sticking to it. Envy immediately possessed her breast. "What!" said she, "has Ali Baba gold so plentiful as to measure it? Whence has he all this wealth?"

Cassim, her husband, was at his counting-house. When he came home his wife said to him, "Cassim, I know you think yourself rich, but Ali Baba is infinitely richer than you. He does not count his money, but measures it." Cassim desired her to explain the riddle, which she did by telling him the stratagem she had used to make the discovery, and showed him the piece of money, which was so old that they could not tell in what prince's reign it was coined.

Cassim, after he had married the rich widow, had never treated Ali Baba as a brother, but scorned and neglected him; and now, instead of being pleased, he conceived a base envy at his brother's prosperity. He could not sleep all that night, and went to him in the morning before sunrise. "Ali Baba," said he, "I am surprised at you! You pretend to be miserably poor, and yet you measure gold. My wife found this at the bottom of the measure you borrowed yesterday."

By this discourse, Ali Baba perceived that Cassim and his wife, through his own wife's folly, knew what they had so much reason to conceal; but what was done could not be undone. Therefore, without showing the least surprise or chagrin, he told all, and offered his brother part of his treasure to keep the secret.

"I expect as much," replied the greedy Cassim haughtily; "but I must know exactly where this treasure is, and how I may visit it

Chapter 3: The Lode Star

myself when I choose; otherwise, I will go and inform against you, and then you will not only get no more, but will lose all you have, and I shall have a share for my information."

Ali Baba told him all he asked, even to the very words he was to use to gain admission into the cave.

Cassim rose the next morning long before the sun, and set out for the forest with ten mules bearing great chests, which he designed to fill, and followed the road which Ali Baba had pointed out to him. It was not long before he reached the rock, and found out the place, by the tree and other marks which his brother had given him. Walking up to the entrance of the cavern, he pronounced the words, "Open, Sesame!" Immediately the door opened, and when he was in, closed upon him.

On examining the cave, his avaricious soul was in transports of delight to find much more riches than he had expected from Ali Baba's relation. Quickly he laid as many bags of gold as he could carry at the door of the cavern; but his thoughts were so full of the great riches he should possess, and how with them he should become the richest money-lender and usurer in the city, that he could not think of the necessary words to make the door open. Instead of "Sesame" he said, "Open, Barley!" and was much amazed to find that the door remained fast shut. He named several sorts of grain, but still the door would not open.

Cassim had never anticipated such a contingency as this, and was so frightened at the danger he was in, that the more he endeavored to remember the word "Sesame," the more his memory was confounded. He threw down the bags he had loaded himself with and walked distractedly up and down the cave, for the first time in his greedy life appreciating that to put your trust in money alone is to pin your faith to the most elusive thing in the world. Yet he had looked to it alone for so long a time that he knew now no other way to turn.

Chapter 3: The Lode Star

About noon the robbers visited their cave. At some distance they saw Cassim's mules straggling about the rock, with great chests on their backs. Alarmed at this, they galloped full speed to the cave, drove away the mules, which strayed through the forest so far that they were soon out of sight, and went directly, with their naked sabres in their hands, to the door, which on their captain pronouncing the proper words, immediately opened.

Cassim, who heard the noise of the horses' feet, at once guessed the arrival of the robbers, and resolved to make one effort for his life. He rushed to the door, and no sooner saw it open, than he ran out and threw the leader down, but could not escape the other robbers, who with their scimeters soon deprived him of life.

There is more to this old Eastern legend, but the meat of it lies here —that if you learn the Magic Secret, the "Open Sesame" of life, wealth and honor are yours for the taking.

But if you become like the greedy Cassim, and get so taken up with the riches that you can think of nothing else—you not only lose the Magic Secret, but you bring down speedy retribution on your head as well.

The "Open, Sesame!"

What is this "Open, Sesame" of life? What is the Philosopher's Stone which turns everything it touches into gold?

It is any controlling idea or desire so intense, so alive and real, that it carries utter faith with it and thus involuntarily establishes a contact with the Holy Spirit within, which attracts to itself everything it needs for its fulfillment.

It is, in short, the Lode Star—the Polar Magnet by means of which we may draw from the heavens above, from the earth beneath or

Chapter 3: The Lode Star

from the waters under the earth anything that is necessary to our controlling idea or desire.

Ridiculous? Stop and think for just a moment.

Have you ever concentrated for days or weeks on the writing of an article or story, on the making of some device, on the discovery of some new formula—on anything that required the deepest thought and faith and concentration?

Remember how there seemed to pour in upon you all sorts of facts and information and material pertinent to the idea you had in mind? Remember how things came to you from the most unlikely and unexpected sources—from the chance words of associates or even strangers; from newspaper and magazine articles, picked up in the most casual way imaginable; from books you happened to see in the windows or in the hands of some friend; from *out of the air,* as it were, unsought, unbidden—except as they were sought out and brought to you by that Mental Magnet within.

The earnest desire for some definite thing, coupled with the sincere belief in your power to get it through the Spirit within, is the most powerful force in the world. As Marie Corelli says in "Life Everlasting":

"Nothing in the universe can resist the force of a steadfastly fixed resolve. What the spirit truly seeks must, by eternal law, be given to it, and what the body needs for the fulfillment of the spirit's demands will be bestowed. From the sunlight and the air and the hidden things of space strength shall be daily and hourly renewed. Everything in nature shall aid in bringing to the resolved soul that which it demands. There is nothing within the circle of creation that can resist its influence. Success, wealth, triumph upon triumph come to every human being who daily 'sets his house in order'—whom no derision can drive from his determined goal, whom no temptation can drag from his appointed course."

Chapter 3: The Lode Star

I know that when I first conceived the idea for this book and began to look for different works of reference to bear out the thought I had in mind, I was almost flooded with material—wonderful material that I had never even heard about, much less knew where to look for. Three of the best works on the subject I have ever seen, literally walked into my office—unsought, unbidden and without cost—and have been of more help to me than anything else I have found. And I am far from being alone in this experience.

In a recent issue of *Advertising and Selling,* Floyd W. Parsons tells how a piece of cheese tossed by one workman at another during the lunch hour missed its mark and dropped into the plating bath used in the production of copper disks from which wax phonograph records were stamped. Later the disks from that bath were found to be far superior to the others, and an investigation revealed that the casein in the cheese had done the trick. This disclosed a possible improvement worth several thousand dollars.

By inadvertently opening the wrong valve, a French scientist found the answer to the long search for liquid oxygen. Again an accident created an industry and gave us an explosive safer and mightier than dynamite.

A great corporation ordered its industrial chemists to produce a paint that could be applied quickly, would dry rapidly, and be tough, hard and resistant to the elements. It had to have some of the properties of glass and yet not crack, and it had to be proof against the action of oil, grease, and acid.

Everything went well up to the point of finding a way to keep the solution in a liquid condition so that it could be applied with a brush. All efforts to solve this problem failed until one day the machinery broke down and the material had to stand for days in the tank until the repairs were completed. When work started again, the chemists were amazed to find that the paint now retained its liquid

Chapter 3: The Lode Star

form. The long-sought secret had finally been discovered, and an accident had again shaped the destiny of a business.

In short, when you have put all of your reasoning, all of your information into the cauldron of thought, there frequently flashes out an idea that is not the logical development of anything you have had before—but a direct inspiration from the Holy Spirit within.

"And thine ears shall hear a word behind thee, saying, This is the way, walk ye in it, when ye turn to the right hand, and when ye turn to the left."—ISAIAH 30:21.

"The key to successful methods," says Thos. A. Edison, "comes right out of the air. A real new thing like a general idea, a beautiful melody, is pulled out of space—a fact which is inexplicable."

Inexplicable? Not at all! It is simply that all knowledge already exists in Divine Mind—in the Father who fills all space and animates all things. There is nothing for us to discover—merely to *seek,* to *unfold.* Columbus did not discover America. It was here all the time. As the Englishman said after three days of traveling on a California-bound train—"How could he have missed it?" Columbus —and all of Europe—merely learned something that Divine Mind had known all the time.

Galileo did not discover that the earth was round; Copernicus did not discover the movement of the planets; Newton did not discover the law of gravitation; any more than your young son discovers the law of mathematics by which 2+2=4. He learns it—yes. He makes the information his own. And to him it partakes of discovery. But the law was known to Divine Mind since time began.

We are God's children, grasping a little at a time of the infinite knowledge He is constantly writing on the blackboard before us—and hailing each bit as a grand discovery of our own. Sir Isaac Newton, one of the greatest geniuses of all time, compared himself

Chapter 3: The Lode Star

to a boy, gathering pebbles on the shore of the vast, unknown ocean of truth.

"God looked down from heaven," said David, "upon the children of men to see if there were any that did understand." —Psalms 14:2.

The great essential is to realize that the Father HAS all information —that the "vast ocean of truth" IS there—and that if we will do our best in the trustful knowledge that the Father *can* and very gladly *will* supply anything beyond our own powers to grasp, our faith and trust will be justified. When God is with us, the impossible becomes possible.

When any problem confronts you that seems beyond your ability to solve, just say to yourself—"I am one with the Infinite Intelligence of the Universe. And Infinite Intelligence HAS the correct answer to this problem. Therefore, I too have the answer, and at the right time and in the right way will manifest it."

There are no new gold deposits. No new diamond fields. All of them have been known to the Father for millions of years.

You don't need to discover anything. You don't need to create something new. All you need to do is to seek the riches and the methods that have been known to the Father for all time. And the place to seek them is not far afield—but in Mind.

A Radio with a Thousand Aerials

Our bodies are, in effect, radio stations powerful or otherwise, as our controlling ideas are strong or weak. The nerves that come to the surface all over our body act as thousands of aerials gathering in impressions from every source. And just as any station properly attuned and powerful enough to "get" it, can pick what it wants out of the air any minute of the day or night, so can you "get" anything you may want—be it riches or success, happiness or health—if

Chapter 3: The Lode Star

your thought be properly keyed and powerful enough to receive it.

For our minds are vast magnets that can attract to us anything we may desire. The only requisite is—they have got to be *charged*. A demagnetized magnet won't draw to it or hold even the weight of a pin. Nor will a demagnetized man attract to himself a single idea or a single penny.

There are two ways of charging your mental magnet:

1. By occasional but heartfelt prayer—like the radio fan who lets his batteries run down until, when something special comes along that he particularly wants, he finds them so weak he can scarcely raise a sound, and forthwith takes himself to the battery man to have them recharged.

2. By praying without ceasing—to go back to the simile of the radio fan again, to attach your batteries to the electric light socket and keep them constantly charged to capacity, ready and able at all times to bring you anything you may wish.

Which method is yours? Old Mother Nature adopts the second. The flowers turn their faces to the sun not just once a day or once a week—but always. The waving grain, the shrubs, the trees, drink in the light and life of the sun every day and all day. They recharge themselves with life and fragrance whenever and as long as opportunity offers.

That is what you too must do. You must first charge the magnet of your mind with a compelling desire. Then keep it recharged with faith in the power and the willingness of the Father to give to you anything of good that may be necessary to the fruition of your prayer. Not only that, but you must realize your ability (through the Father) to draw to yourself anything of good. In short, you must realize your Sonship with God, and the consequent fact that all of good is already yours—that God has done his part—that it is up to

Chapter 3: The Lode Star

you merely to manifest, to unfold, to SEE the good things that the Father has provided for you in such profusion.

When Hagar and Ishmael were wandering in the desert, and could find no water and seemed about to perish, then Hagar cried aloud to the Lord.

"And God heard the voice of the lad; and the angel of God called to Hagar out of heaven, and said unto her, What aileth thee, Hagar? Fear not; for God hath heard the voice of the lad where he is.
"And God opened her eyes, and she saw a well of water; and she went, and filled the bottle with water, and gave the lad drink."—Genesis 21:17, 19.

Again, when the three kings in the desert sought water for their men and horses, the Prophet Elisha told them: "Thus saith the Lord—Ye shall not see wind, neither shall ye see rain, yet make this valley full of ditches." — II Kings, 13:16-17.

And though it looked a hopeless task, the three kings set their men to work as directed, and after they had prepared the ditches, the rains came and filled them.
Wherever you are and whatever you need, supply is always there—for supply is in the Father, and the Father is everywhere. It is like the air we breathe—it is all around us, always available, always plentiful—unless we lock ourselves into the airtight houses of limitation.

The trouble is that we have for so long been taught that everything of good must be fought for, struggled for, taken away from someone else, that we can't believe when we are told that all we need do is to open up the windows of our souls and let in the Holy Spirit—open up the channels of supply and let riches flow freely to us. To quote Trench's beautiful poem

Chapter 3: The Lode Star

"Make channels for the stream of love,
Where they may broadly run,
For Love has overflowing streams
To fill them every one;

But if at any time we cease
Such channels to provide,
The very founts of Love for us,
Will soon be parched and dried;

For we must share if we would keep
Such blessings from above,
Ceasing to give, we cease to have,
Such is the law of Love."

We see others breathing deeply of the air about us, and we don't begrudge them it because we know there is plenty for all. We see others enjoying the sunlight; the clear water from the spring; and we rejoice with them in it. But let another make a lot of money, and immediately we become envious, for we think he has made it that much harder for us to get any.

The best things in life, the greatest essentials to life, are free. Air, sunshine, water— all are free, because the supply of them is inexhaustible.

What we fail to realize is that there is just as inexhaustible supply of the things that money will buy as there is of sunlight or water or air. And they can be drawn just as freely from the Father through the magic of faith and a compelling idea.

But you can't do it if you dam up the source of supply with doubts and fears. You must not limit supply as did the widow in the Scriptural story. Left destitute, her creditors were pressing her hard; and her sons, as was the law in that day, were to become bondsmen

Chapter 3: The Lode Star

for the debt she owed. In her distress she came to the prophet Elisha, and he asked—"What have you in your house?" She replied—"I have nothing but a vessel of oil." He said—"Send out to your neighbors and borrow all the vessels you can; take them empty into a room, and pour into them the oil which you have." She did not question him but did as she was told; she poured the oil from the vessel which contained all that she possessed and filled all those which she had borrowed. Then she told her sons to get others, but they said—"We have no more." And as soon as they made that announcement, the oil stopped flowing—not one drop came after all the vessels were full—II Kings 4:2-6. Do you see who determined the quantity that should come to the widow? Was it God? I know your answer—"It was the woman herself." She received just the amount for which she had made preparation.

It's Not the Supply That Is Limited—It Is Ourselves!

Too many of us are like the little colored boy and the watermelon. An old gentleman, seeing the difficulty the boy was having in storing away so large a melon, stopped and asked, "Too much melon, isn't it, son?" "No, suh!" replied the youngster with conviction, "just not enough niggah."

Why does so large a part of humanity suffer hunger and want?

Certainly not from lack on the part of old Mother Earth. Ask the farmers and they will tell you their trouble is overproduction—not scarcity. Ask the scientists, and they will tell you that there is food in plenty in the very air. And not only food but power and riches. Ask the miners—whether of gold, or silver, or diamonds, or coal, or iron—and they will tell you that the supply exceeds the demand. Go to the manufacturer and ask him—and again your answer will be the same.

Evidently there is plenty to go around. Evidently the Father has not failed us, any more than he fails the birds of the air or the beasts of

Chapter 3: The Lode Star

the field, in providing the supply. The problem is merely one of our ability to receive—to receive and digest and distribute and exchange.

There is plenty for all—of everything of good. The poor are hungry, the needy are in lack, not because there is not enough supply, but because their mental magnets have become so weak through discouragement, their channels so stopped up with fear and worry, that the stream of supply no longer reaches them.

If you cut your finger, what happens? You call upon your heart for an extra supply of blood to rebuild the damaged part. And the heart immediately responds.

If you have urgent need of money or other worldly goods, what should you do? Call upon the Heart of all things to send you an extra supply for your emergency—and He will just as promptly and cheerfully respond.

There's a little comedy on one of the Broadway stages that illustrates this idea clearly. A couple of young darkies are boxing—the first, an active, alert little fellow, on the go every minute—the second a tall, shambling, lazy sort, slow-moving, slow-thinking.

The big one is too lazy to really fight his active opponent. He contents himself with trying to guard himself. But every time he moves a hand, the little one gets in a punch.

Finally the big one catches hold of the little fellow by the shoulders, holds him off at arm's length and studies him for a minute. Then he puts one hand in the other's face and lets the little one jab at him, the while he holds him off at arm's length.

The little one swings and punches, but his arms are too short. He can't quite reach the big fellow. The lazy one throws back his head and laughs as he prepares to swing his good right arm at leisure.

Chapter 3: The Lode Star

"That's all I wanted to know," he says.

And all you need to know when that little devil of fear or worry or lack assails you and you want to hold him off for a while until you can swing your good right arm to put him out for the count, is that the answer to any trouble, the remedy for any lack, the antidote for any ill is just around the corner. Charge your mental magnet with earnest desire and faith—and the need does not exist which you cannot satisfy.

"The Lord's hand is not shortened, that it cannot save," promised the Prophet Isaiah
59:1. "Neither His ear heavy, that it cannot hear."

The principal reason there is so much truth in the Scriptural quotation—"To him that hath shall be given," is that the man who has a tidy sum safely put away loses all worry about supply. Like the darkey in the play, he feels that his money gives him that bit of extra reach with which he can easily fend off the attacks of want and fear and worry, while he is getting in his good licks elsewhere. True, he places his dependence upon money rather than upon the Spirit, but the belief that he has money enough not to have to worry emboldens him to demand more. He loses all sense of fear. He expects and demands only the *good* things of life—and consequently the good things of life come to him. To put it in the words of Solomon—"He that hath a bountiful eye shall be blessed"—Proverbs 22:9.

Remember the story of the merchant who saw ruin staring him in the face unless he could raise money immediately? He went to a wise friend, who gave him a great nugget of gold—on condition, however, that he was not to use it except as a last resource.

Knowing that he had the gold to use at need, the merchant went boldly about his business with a mind at ease—faced his creditors so confidently that they gladly trusted him further—with the result

Chapter 3: The Lode Star

that he never needed to use the gold.

But you don't need to go to the pages of fiction for such examples. Most of us have seen similar instances ourselves. There is the classic case of George Muller, of Bristol, England, who maintained orphanages which spent millions, through which hundreds of children were rescued from the slums and fitted for places of trust in the world—*all without any visible means of support!*

Like the oil from the widow's cruse, the money came through his perfect faith in the Giver of all good. Many and many a time utter penury stared him in the face, so that any man of less Job-like faith would have been discouraged. Once hundreds of hungry children sat waiting for their breakfasts—and there was not a mouthful to give them.

But always in time—though sometimes at the very last moment—his faith was justified and some generous donation would supply all their wants. Like Job, he might well have said—"I know that my Redeemer liveth."—Job 19:25. "Though He slay me, yet will I trust in Him."—Job 13:15.

Or with David—"Yea, though I walk through the valley of the shadow of Death I shall fear no evil, for Thou art with me."—Psalms 23:4.

For nothing stands between you and the dearest wish of your heart but doubt and fear. When you can pray without doubting, when you can believe as the Master bade us believe—"Whatsoever ye ask for when ye pray, believe that ye RECEIVE it and ye SHALL HAVE IT"—every desire of your heart will be instantly filled.

What, then, is the "Open, Sesame," of life? What is the Magic Secret that will bring to you everything of good you may wish?

It is simply a "Message to Garcia." There is within you a Holy

Chapter 3: The Lode Star

Spirit who is your part of Divinity—who knows all, sees all and can do all things. Give him a definite task, magnetize Him with your absolute belief in His ability and His readiness to accomplish it—charge Him with such absolute faith that you can actually SEE HIM DOING IT—and "as thy faith is, so it will be unto you." The Spirit within you can draw from the heavens or the earth or the waters under the earth whatever you may need for the consummation of your desires.

How do men talk 3,000 miles across the Atlantic—without wires, without cables? In the Marconi beam system, they do it by focusing the electric waves into one great beam, just as a searchlight focuses all the light waves into one powerful ray. Ordinary broadcasting stations let their waves radiate in all directions like the ripples a pebble makes in a pool of water. The Marconi beam system focuses them all into one powerful beam and then directs it straight across the Atlantic, with the result that they will carry your message wherever you wish it to go.

Focus your desires in the same way. Instead of frittering away your energy in a thousand directions, bring them all to bear in one powerful beam on one single desire at a time. Do that, and you can attract to yourself anything of good you may wish.

So what do you want?

Is it money? Then know that the Father is the source of all wealth. Go to Him—tell Him your need—ask Him for money in abundance to meet your needs. Bless the money you now have—know that the Father is in it even as he is in all good things— then see it, in your mind's eye, *multiplied*.

Send forth the Holy Spirit within you to the source of supply for as much as you need or can use to good advantage. Then SEE HIM DRAWING THAT SUPPLY! See a golden stream flowing to you in the sunlight, in the moonbeams!

Chapter 3: The Lode Star

Actually speak the word that sends your Spirit forth. Tell Him — "Holy Spirit, you know that the one Law of Supply is abundance —plenty for every right purpose, plenty for every right desire. You know that the Father has all of abundance, that there is unlimited money available for me right now, that as His son I am heir to it. Go you, therefore, bring to me of the infinite abundance that is mine, all that I may need for this purpose. If there is anything you wish *me* to do, give me a definite lead."

Speak the word, then cast your burden upon the Holy Spirit—and forget it! "My word shall not return unto me void, but shall accomplish that where unto it is sent."—Isaiah 55:11. Every doubt, every fear, every worry that you entertain is a shackle holding Him back. If you can release Him from all dominion of the conscious mind, if you can have the faith in Him that you have when you give a task to a trusted servant and thereafter look upon it as done—depend upon it, He will bring you what you ask for.

But it is so hard for us to let go. We are like a man on a desert isle, daily releasing our one carrier pigeon with a message for help, yet as often bringing him back to earth again by the string on his foot that we are too distrustful to untie.

Yet when at last in desperation we do cut off the shackles, our faithful messenger flies straight home with his message of need and brings succor to us immediately.

That is why so often our prayers are not answered until the eleventh hour. We won't turn loose the string. We won't trust entirely in the Spirit. We think He needs our help, too. When all that we need is a little trust.

It is the same no matter what you may want. Are you seeking a position? Know that in the Mind of the Father there is one right

Chapter 3: The Lode Star

position for you—one position that in the present stage of your development is best fitted for you even as you are best fitted for it. You have a definite place in the great scheme of things. And there is one right position that marks the next step in your forward progress.

That position IS yours. You have only to *know* this and to realize it. Then send forth the Spirit within you to bring that position to you or you to it. *Speak the word.* Throw the burden upon Him, asking Him only, if there is anything you can do to forward the work, to give you a definite lead. Then rest content in the knowledge that the Spirit is doing the work.

"Prove me now herewith, saith the Lord of Hosts, if I will not open you the windows of heaven, and pour you out a blessing that there shall not be room enough to receive it."—Malachi 3:10.

What, then, is the answer? Is this a lazy-man's world, where all that one needs to do is to fast and pray?

By no means! It is a worker's world—and the only ones who ever get anything out of it that is worthwhile are the workers. Mere wishing never magnetized the Spirit within to bring anything of good.

Look at all of Nature—busy every moment, never idle—*but never worrying.* Model after her. Whatever it is you may want, remember that you must get it first in Mind. See yourself with it there—see yourself receiving it. Make it as real as you can. Be thankful for it!

Then set about manifesting that dream in the material world. Do anything you can think of that will help to bring it about. Concentrate your thought upon it in every conceivable way. But never worry as to the outcome. Know that after you have done all that is possible for you to do—if you are still lacking in some essential, you can sit back in the utter confidence that the Holy

Chapter 3: The Lode Star

Spirit within will supply that lack. Give of your best—and you need never fear for the outcome. Your best will come back to you—amplified a hundredfold.

"Ye know in all your hearts and in all your souls, that not one thing hath failed of all the good things which the Lord your God spake concerning you; all are come to pass unto you, and not one thing hath failed thereof."—Joshua 23:14.

Chapter 4: The Man of Brass

AWAY back in the 13th century, there lived a scientist so far ahead of his times that he had to record most of his discoveries in cypher —to keep from being burned at the stake.

Even as it was, he was thought by the ignorant to be a sorcerer, a magician, an apostate who had sold his soul to the devil. Only among the initiate was he known as "The Wonderful Doctor."

His name was Roger.

And wonderful he truly was. Many of the chemical formulas he discovered are in use today. He made gunpowder. He discovered the possibilities of the magnifying glass. He was a forerunner of Galileo and Copericus.

Innumerable legends grew up about him, some of which will be touched upon in the later volumes of this Course—notably his "Elixir of Life." But the most persistent of these legends deals with "The Man of Brass."

Roger, you must know, had mastered seven different languages in his efforts to wrest from every possible source the secrets of science that had been known to previous ages. Among these languages was the Arabic. And one day there was brought to him an old Arabic manuscript which some wandering knight had picked up in far-away Palestine.

Roger read the work and marveled. It told first how to fashion a man of brass. Then, by means of clockwork and wires leading to certain jars of chemicals (the first crude storage batteries), how the eyeballs could be made to glow, the tongue to move, smoke to issue from the nostrils, and noise from the mouth. But most important of all—how, by adhering to certain directions, the Man of Brass could

Chapter 4: The Man of Brass

be made to speak *and reveal a secret of the utmost importance to every Englishman.*

For seven years, Roger toiled over his Man of Brass. He is reputed to have spent a fortune in scientific experiments, and no small part of it must have gone into this brazen image. At last it was finished. Everything had been done with the greatest care, strictly in accordance with the directions given in the manuscript.

Then he sat down and waited. For more than a month, there was never a minute when Roger or his friend and confidante Friar Bungay was not sitting before the brazen image, listening for any sound it might utter. But neither friars nor philosophers can keep on without sleep.

One night, when Friar Bungay had gone home, Roger was nodding in his chair before the image. "If I can keep awake but a few hours longer," he muttered, "the wonderful voice will speak and the great secret will be known." But he could not keep awake. His eyes would close in spite of himself. Finally he called his servant, admonished him to wake him immediately if the image should speak and went off to snatch a bit of rest. The servant sat near the door, his eyes fastened in frightened fascination upon those of the image, his fingers gripped about the cudel in his hands.

Suddenly the eyes of the image glowed, its lips moved and in a whisper there issued from its mouth the words—
"TIME IS!"
The servant jumped to his feet and started to run, but as the brazen image seemed to remain rooted to the one spot, he paused on the threshold to see what more it might have to say.

Presently again the eyes lighted up, the lips moved, and a voice like the rattling of a kettle-drum shrilled out—

"TIME WAS!"

Chapter 4: The Man of Brass

This time the servant all but fled. But before he could get the door open, the eyes glowed once more and in a voice of thunder there issued the words—

"TIME IS PAST!"

And with that the image fell and smashed into a thousand pieces.

Roger is said to have been so bitterly disappointed at what he considered the wasting of all his seven years of labor that he burned his books, closed his study and spent the rest of his life in a monastery.

But had his work been wasted? Is there any secret of greater importance than the knowledge that—*"Time is NOW?* Most of us are so busy regretting the past or planning what we are going to be and do in some far distant day or state that we overlook the chances for happiness and success that are all around us now.

The past is gone and done with. No amount of regrets will bring it back. So let us forget it—except in so far as we may draw lessons from it. Let our motto be "Yesterday ended last night."

As for the future—it is still ahead of us, and no man may tell what it holds.

But the present is ours to do with as we will. So let us live it to the utmost. *"Time IS"*—not has been or will be. "Time *passes"*—you will never have one bit more of time than you have this minute.

So what do you want to do with it? What have you to ask of the Father of Life—not next year, or ten years from now, or in some indefinite future state— but NOW?

There's an old Eastern legend that the gates of Paradise are opened

Chapter 4: The Man of Brass

only once in each thousand years. And judging by most people's attitude toward life, that belief seems to have obtained credence among us, for most of us look forward to happiness and success as something in the far distant future. We pray—but look for the result of our prayers in some vague future state.

All of supply is already in existence. Why put off drawing upon it six months—or a year—or ten years? Why not charge the magnet of your mind to draw from Infinite Supply what you may want NOW?

"I cause those that love me to inherit substance, and I will fill their treasures."— Proverbs 8:21.

If you were to take a vote of the Christian peoples of the world, you would find them practically unanimous in believing that God intended to save their souls in the next world—but that in so far as their present existence is concerned, you've got to leave Him out of the reckoning!

Yet if you took from the Scriptures, all those parts that tell of His succoring those in trouble—not in some far-off future state, but in this life; if you left out all His promises of protection and reward here on earth to those that loved Him and kept His commandments —how much of the Bible would there be left?

"And the Lord shall guide thee continually, and satisfy thy soul in drought, and make fat thy bones; and thou shalt be like a watered garden, and like a spring of water whose waters fail not."—Isaiah 58:11.

If only all could realize that even in the heart of the humblest laborer, of the poorest scrubwoman, lies the key to riches inexhaustible, what a world of poverty and misery we might avoid.

Most of us find it easy enough to believe this when our pockets are

Chapter 4: The Man of Brass

full and all is going well with us. But let the wolf start scratching at the door and then watch us. Yet that is the very time when we most need faith! The fact is that we have more confidence in the weekly pay-envelope, uncertain as it is, than we have in the Almighty!

Consider the lilies of the field. Consider the birds; the denizens of the field; of the forest; of the air and the water; they don't lack for what they need. The big difference between them and you is that you have been given free will. You don't need to go to the Father unless you wish. You can struggle and toil on your own account. You can look upon this as a vale of tears—and find it so. Or you can do your best—and then rest in the arms of the Father while "He doeth the works."

"Yea, the Almighty shall be thy defence, and thou shall have plenty of silver,"—Job 22:25.

All that you need, all of good that you want, is right at your hand.

"The soul answers never by words," says Emerson, "but by the thing itself sought after."

Have you ever seen the Hopi Indians' Snake Dance—their prayer for rain? It is probably the oldest religious ceremony on this continent, and it is said that it never yet has failed to bring the rains.

"Speak to him thou, for he heareth
When Spirit with Spirit doth meet,
Closer is he than breathing,
And nearer than hand and feet."

Scientists may talk learnedly of atmospheric conditions and natural laws, but the fact remains—the Indians send up their heartfelt prayers to the Holy Spirit in simple faith—and so far as is known, the rains have never failed to promptly come!

Chapter 4: The Man of Brass

"Whither shall I go from thy Spirit?" cried the Psalmist of old, "Or whither shall I flee from Thy presence? If I ascend up into heaven Thou are there; if I make my bed in hell, behold Thou are there. If I take the wings of the morning and dwell in the uttermost parts of the sea; even there shall Thy hand lead me and Thy right hand shall hold me. If I say, Surely the darkness shall cover me; even the night shall be light about me."—Psalms 139:7-11.

There is in this universe a Power that hears the cry of the human heart. There is behind us a Father "whose good pleasure it is to give us the Kingdom." You don't have to beg Him for the good things of life any more than you have to beg the sun for its heat. You have only to draw near and take of the bountiful supply He is constantly holding out to you.

So what is it you want of the Father of Life? A house? A toy? A car? Success in this or that undertaking? Health? Love? Happiness?

Whatever it is, you can have it. Whatever of good you ask for with earnest desire and simple faith, the Father will gladly give.

So have no hesitancy in going to Him about little things. Don't you suppose He is as glad to see you clothed in a new suit or new dress as He is to see the birds preening their new feathers, the wild things of the forest in their shining new coat, the snake and his like in their new skins? Don't you suppose it gives Him as much pleasure to give you something you have been longing for as it gladdens the heart of an earthly father to give a much-desired toy to his little boy?

"Thou openest thy hand and satisfieth the desire of every living thing."

I have had people write me that prayer has brought to them such simple little things as flowers, as toys for the children, as an

Chapter 4: The Man of Brass

automobile. Last Christmas one reader wrote me that he had needed $500. That he had put his problem before the Father confidently, believingly. Then left it with Him. To use his own words, "The $500 came from so unexpected a source that if the President himself had sent it to him, he would not have been more surprised."

"No good things will He withhold from them that walketh uprightly."

The very fact that you have some earnest desire is the best evidence that the answer to that desire is in the great heart of God.

"Time is NOW!"

That earnest desire of yours is in the present. And the supply is just as much so. The Father is just as much present here and now as He will ever be. So why put off the realization of your desires to some vague and distant future? Why not realize them in the now?

What is it that you want?

Whatever it is, it already exists somewhere, in some form. And if your desire be strong enough, your faith great enough, you can attract it to you.

There are riches in abundance for you. They already exist. They are labeled YOURS in the mind of the Father. And until you get them, they will remain idle. You don't have to take them from someone else. You don't have to envy anyone else what he has. All you have to KNOW is that somewhere all of riches that you can ever desire are lying waiting for you.

Don't try to get them all at once.

If you had a million dollars on deposit in some bank, you wouldn't rush there and draw it out, to carry around with you or to hide about

Chapter 4: The Man of Brass

the house. No—as long as you had confidence in the integrity of the bank, you would leave your money on deposit there, drawing upon it merely as you needed it.

Have you less confidence in the Bank of the Father than in those of man? Must you ask It for all your heritage at once for fear the Bank will fail? Or can you ask each day for that day's needs—"Give us this day our daily bread"—in the simple faith that our every draft will be met promptly, fully, no matter what the size?

The man who has that simple faith will not try to pinch pennies. He won't "pass by on the other side" when a worthy need approaches him.

He will spend cheerfully—for any right purpose. He will bless the money he sends out, putting it to work in the confident knowledge that when used gainfully, it will come back increased and multiplied.

The same thing applies to your home, to your surroundings. There is a perfect home for you already built in the Father's mind. Know this—realize it—then, like Hagar in the wilderness, pray that your eyes may be opened that you may SEE this perfect home that is yours.

There is a perfect position for you. A perfect mate. A perfect work. A perfect idea of each cell and organism in your body. In later volumes of this set, I shall try to show you how through the promises of the Scriptures these may all be realized. Suffice it now to say that they all exist in the Father's mind. It is up to you merely to seek that you may find them.

You have the most powerful magnet on earth right within your own mind. Uncover it! Charge it with desire and faith. Speak the word that sends the Holy Spirit that is within you in quest of what you wish. Then cast the burden upon Him and thereafter look upon your

Chapter 4: The Man of Brass

desire as an accomplished fact.

"Whatsoever ye ask for when ye pray, believe that ye *receive* it and ye shall have it."

Prepare for the thing you have asked for, even though there be not the slightest sign of its coming. Act the part! Like the three Kings in the desert, dig your ditches to receive the water, even though there be not a cloud in the sky. And your ditches will be filled—even as were theirs.
"Be still—and know that I am God!" Wait calmly, confidently, in the full assurance that the Father has what you want and will gladly give it to you.

One's ships come in over a calm sea.

The Law of Karma

You have probably heard of the Law of Karma. It is Sanskrit, you know, for "Comeback." It is one of the oldest laws known to man—yet perhaps the least regarded.

It is the law of the boomerang. In the parlance of today, it is—"Chickens come home to roost." Even in science we find it, as Newton's Third Law of Motion—"Action and reaction are always equal to each other."

Wherein does this law affect us now? Only in that, if you wish riches, if you long for happiness, health, success, you must think abundance, you must charge your mind with happy thoughts, healthy thoughts, optimistic thoughts.

If you are seeking riches, you will never get them by stopping up all the avenues of outgo, and waiting for your vessel to fill up from the top. I remember one man who wrote me from down in West Virginia that when he received *The Secret of the Ages* he was a

Chapter 4: The Man of Brass

farmhand, working for $1 a day. Through the confidence and knowledge acquired through the books, he had landed a job at $6.20 a day of eight hours, where before he had labored for twelve hours on the farm. But, he wrote, "I've returned the books. You gave me time to get out of them what I wanted and return at your expense without buying them. I think now I can make a million. So I don't want to spend any money now. I want to make my million." That man was like a funnel—big at the receiving end, but little at the outgoing part. The Law of Karma will get him before he has gone far. You have got to cast your bread upon the waters, in the secure confidence that it will come back to you multiplied a hundredfold.

If you are longing for a beautiful home, you will never get it by thinking thoughts of poverty and lack. Forget the state of your pocketbook. Your supply is not there. All supply is in the Father, "with Whom is no variableness nor shadow of turning." So go to the Father with your desire. Try to picture in your mind's eye the perfect home that already is yours in Divine Mind. Make it complete in every detail. Realize that this perfect home is yours—that it already exists—in the mind of the Father. Then send forth the Holy Spirit to bring it to you or you to it.

Don't ask for some particular house. Ask, if you wish, for one like it. Don't try to take that which is another's. Know that the one perfect home for you already exists in Divine Mind, even though you may never have seen it. Then leave it to the Holy Spirit to manifest it.

Speak the word—then cast the burden upon the Holy Spirit within. The Father sends His gifts in His own way, even as earthly fathers frequently do. Make all preparations for them—dig your ditches—open up the windows of your soul. Be ready to receive.

Remember, in Genesis I: 1-2—"In the beginning, God created the heaven and the earth. And the earth was without form and void; and

Chapter 4: The Man of Brass

darkness was upon the face of the deep. *And the Spirit of God moved upon the face of the waters."*

That Spirit of God still moves upon the face of the waters. And upon the face of the land. That Spirit of God is the Holy Spirit within you. And just as He helped to form the earth from the void, so will He bring form to your dreams, your desires. If only you do your part. If only you have the faith. If only you can cast the burden upon Him—confidently, believingly!

"Oh Judah, fear not; but tomorrow go out against them, for the Lord will be with you. You shall not need to fight this battle; set yourselves, stand you still, *and see the salvation of the Lord with you."*
And the time to do it is NOW.

Chapter 5: Start Something!

A Spanish adventurer gets together a following of a couple of thousand out-at-elbows soldiers of fortune like himself—and with them conquers a nation! A disciplined, well-led warlike nation numbering millions! Defeats armies ten times the size of his little force, time after time! Captures a walled city garrisoned by a great army and protected by dykes and canals, and makes its emperor prisoner!

I refer to Hernando Cortez, conqueror of Mexico.

Another Spaniard, with a handful of followers, enslaves the whole of Peru, carries away the vast treasures of the Incas, and makes Spain the richest nation on the globe!

That was 400 years ago, but it is easy enough to find their counterparts today. A few years ago Persia had been almost dismembered by Russia and England. And Reza Khan was but a poor trooper in the Persian army. Today Persia has been restored to an independent state—and Reza Khan is its Ruler.

Before the war Mussolini was an unknown Socialist worker; during the war, a common soldier. Today he is head of a re-nationalized Italy.

Ebert, a saddle-maker before the war—becomes President of the new German Republic. Trotsky, a waiter in a cheap New York restaurant—is made War Minister of Soviet Russia. Mustapha Kemal, a good soldier—but until the war unknown—makes himself Ruler of Turkey. Every day brings its grist of new stars in the world firmament—new and comet-like rises to fame.

How do they do it? What is the secret behind such phenomenal successes?

Chapter 5: Start Something!

Not education—many of these men had no education to speak of. Not training—none of them was ever trained for real leadership. Then what is it?

Just one thing these men all had in common—the daring to *start something!*

If Cortez had been content to sit around in Cuba and wait for something to turn up, do you suppose we should ever have heard of him?

If Reza Khan had been content to do his mere duty as a Persian trooper; if Mussolini had sat down and rested on his laurels as a soldier; if Ebert had been satisfied to keep on making saddles; if Mustapha Kemal had merely obeyed whatever orders he received; do you suppose their countrymen would have started out on a still hunt for them, routed them out of their obscurity and put them at the head of their governments?
Not in a thousand years!

You may—and do—possess latent ability equal to any man on earth; you have ready to your call, through the Holy Spirit within you, not merely the wisdom of a Solomon but the Wisdom of God! Yet all of this will not get you anywhere—all of this will never result in the world calling upon you to lead it—*unless you use it to start something!*

"Bubbles"

You know the air castles a young fellow builds when he is planning his future with his Best Girl. You know what pictures of wonderful achievement he can paint for her. The wealth of the Indies is but a trifle compared with the fortune he is going to lay at her feet.

"Day dreams," we call them—and laugh good-naturedly at the

Chapter 5: Start Something!

fondness of youth and love for believing in such bubbles, such figments of the imagination. But these dreams are very real and very dear to every boy—and girl. They embody all those things they hope some day soon to see materialize.

The only trouble with them is, that with most of us these bubbles are so soon pricked. We meet with discouragement. The fine point of our enthusiasm and ambition is blunted. Soon we lapse into a regular grind, and the man we hoped to be, the man we painted in such glowing terms to our Sweetheart—the man she really married—quietly passes out, leaving nothing but the husk of what might have been.

Is it any wonder there are so many unhappy marriages, when you compare the realities a man actually gives to the girl who marries him, with the "Bubbles" he promised her before?

The wonder is that so many girls shed only a few tears over their shattered dreams, forget their disillusionment, and knuckle down to the tiresome, dispiriting daily round of cooking and housework—of tending babies and being good wives to their plodding husbands.

The greatest waste in business today is the waste of the enthusiasm of all the fine young fellows that go into it. True—their enthusiasm is frequently misdirected—but that is *your* opportunity. Go look at Niagara Falls!

For uncounted years the Niagara River dashed over its rocky cliff, the power of millions of horses behind it—a beautiful sight for the occasional tourist —but nothing more!

Today that same Niagara turns the wheels of a hundred great industries—gives light and power to all of Western New York—is soon to become the basis of a giant superpower system for the entire Northeast.
What made the difference? The Niagara has not changed—it had

Chapter 5: Start Something!

exactly the same power afore-time. 'Tis simply that man has learned how to *direct* that power, to use that energy for useful purposes.

"Give instruction to a wise man, and he will be yet wiser," says the Proverbs (9); "teach a just man, and he will increase in learning."

Remember the story of the young King of the Black Isles? He started out full of high ambitions. But the wicked enchantress (Lack of Initiative) turned him into black marble from the waist down. So he was condemned to sit in his palace and bemoan his fate until there came a new King to lift the spell, to inspire him for high emprise, to keep him from ever again lapsing into the state of half man and half statue.

"And Moses said unto the Lord, O my Lord, I am not eloquent, neither heretofore, nor since thou hast spoken unto thy servant: but I am slow of speech, and of a slow tongue.

"And the Lord said unto him, Who hath made man's mouth? Or who maketh the dumb, or deaf, or the seeing, or the blind? Have not I the Lord?

"Now therefore go, and I will be with thy mouth, and teach thee what thou shalt say."

The world's most tragic figure is the man who never starts anything. He is dead from the waist down. He sits and wishes and dreams; he goes through motions, doing routine things that a machine could do just as well, but he never gets anywhere.

How did Carnegie make his millions? By finding a new way to make steel—and then starting to *do* it! How did Woolworth, how did Penny, make their successes? By trying out new methods of merchandising—by starting something. How did Ford become the richest man in the world? By visioning the new transportation

Chapter 5: Start Something!

within the reach of everyone—and then starting to put it there!

You want to get out of the rut—to grow—to develop into something better. And there are unnumbered new methods in industry, new inventions, new ideas—waiting merely to be uncovered.

To whom will these prizes go? Nine times out of ten to the man who starts something—to the man who dreams great dreams, and then has the courage, the belief in himself, in his Spirit, in his Destiny, to make the start, to take the plunge, *to go!*

"And the Spirit of the Lord shall rest upon him, the spirit of wisdom and understanding, the spirit of counsel and might, the spirit of knowledge and of the fear of the Lord."—Isaiah II.

The Things That Can't Be Done

When John MacDonald first proposed to build the great New York subways, people laughed at him. He went to one "big" financier after another, and the answer of all was the same. "Dig a tunnel under all these streets and houses, with their maze of pipe lines and electric cables and gas mains and sewers? Impossible!"

But through it all he held to the one main idea. "You have a cellar under your house, haven't you?" he asked them. "And you dug it without much trouble, didn't you? Well, I'm not thinking of building a tunnel the length of this island. I'm planning to dig a string of cellars—*and then connect them together!*"

And he finally found a man big enough to see the idea—and to back it.

"Thou shalt make thy prayer unto Him, and He shall hear thee, and thou shalt pay thy vows.

Chapter 5: Start Something!

"Thou shalt also decree a thing, and it shall be established unto thee: and the light shall shine upon thy ways."—Job 22:27-28.

In this day of miracles, it would be a hardy spirit that would say that anything is impossible. The time is not far distant when men will harness the tides, get motive power and much of their food from the air and from the tropic seas, talk to anyone anywhere and see them while they talk. These and a thousand other inventions even more wonderful are in the very air. Why shouldn't you be the one to start some of them?

You don't need to be an engineer. You don't need to be an inventor. Pasteur was not a doctor, yet he did more for medical science than any doctor. Whitney was not a cotton planter. Not even a Southerner. He was a Connecticut schoolteacher. Yet he invented the cotton gin! Bell was a professor of elocution, and he once said that he invented the telephone because he knew nothing of electricity. He didn't know it couldn't be done! Morse, of telegraphic fame, was a portrait painter—not an electrician. Dunlop (maker of tires) was a veterinary surgeon. Gillette was a traveling salesman. Eastman a bank clerk. Ingersoll a mechanic. Harriman a broker. Gary a lawyer.

In fact, most of the great inventors and pioneers have been outsiders. Why? They don't know the things that can't be done—*so they go ahead and do them!*

"Opportunity," says Doc Lane, "is as scarce as oxygen; men fairly breathe it and do not know it."

It is not necessary to have a "pull" to succeed. In fact, a "pull" is more often than not just that—a pull backward. What we need is the "push" of necessity. For most of us are so constituted that, unless we have to put into the fight all our strength and energy, we just jog along in a slothful, ambitionless sort of way, getting nowhere.

Chapter 5: Start Something!

The saving event in many a man's life has been the blow that knocked the props out from under him and left him to look out for himself. As Emerson put it: "It is only as a man puts off all foreign support and stands alone that I see him firm and to prevail. He is weaker by every recruit to his banner."

So never envy the man with a "pull." Pity him. He has lost the greatest thing there is in business—the need for individual initiative.

You say you have to start at the bottom, while Bill Smith's father left him enough money to begin at the head of a real business? Never mind. Start something—even if it be only a peanut stand—and ten years from now you will have not only some very valuable experience, but a business that will be paying you dividends and give you an insurance for the future. Whereas the chances are that though Bill Smith may have the experience, that is all he will have. Most of the big businesses of today, you know, started on a shoestring.

"Thus saith the Lord; Refrain thy voice from weeping, and thine eyes from tears: for thy work shall be rewarded, saith the Lord."—Jeremiah 31.

Democracy is equality, not of place, but of opportunity. Just because you were born on Fifth Avenue doesn't mean that you are going to stay there. And just because you were born on the East Side doesn't mean that you have got to stay there. Al Smith is but one of thousands who have come up from humble surroundings to the topmost rung of the ladder of success.

"Always the real leaders of men," says Dr. Frank Crane, "the real kings, have come up from the common people. The finest flowers in the human flora grow in the woods pasture and not in the hothouse; no privileged class, no Royal house, no carefully selected

Chapter 5: Start Something!

stock produced a Leonardo or a Michelangelo in art, a Shakespeare or Burns in letters, a Galli Curci or Paderewski in music, a Socrates or Kant in philosophy, an Edison or Pasteur in science, a Wesley or a Knox in religion."

The Law of Compensation is constantly at work. When men grow to put too much dependence upon the fortune or the institution or the position that has been given them, these props are suddenly removed. When through grim necessity they have learned not to rely upon anything short of the Infinite, the channels of supply are reopened to them.

"Put not your trust in Princes," advised the Psalmist. Not because Princes are so much more unreliable than ordinary men, but because they are mere tributaries—even as you are—to the King of Kings.
Put not your trust in some other man or institution. Go direct to the Fount! Don't tap some other man's channel. Go direct to the main Source of Supply!

"By me kings reign, and princes decree justice.

"By me princes rule, and nobles, even all the judges of the earth.

"I love them that love me; and those that seek me early shall find me.

"Riches and honour are with me; durable riches and righteousness."
—Proverbs 8:15-19.

Be King in Your Own Thoughts

"Every man," says a mediaeval writer, "has within him the making of a great saint." And every one of us has in him the making of a great success.

Chapter 5: Start Something!

"Less than a year ago," reads a letter to me from W. Bruce Haughton, "I started in the automotive business in Jacksonville with $23.00 in my pocket. I bought $14.40 worth of tools and rented a two-car garage in the back yard of the house where I rented a room. I then went to several of the city professional men and told them what I could do for their cars. In thirty days I had a net return of $476.80 with an overhead of about $50.00.

"In June, 1926, I had to find bigger quarters to handle my business, for I then had 591 regular customers coming to my 'Back Yard' for service they could not buy elsewhere. Today I am negotiating with a concern for another corner in the best part of this city to handle my patrons who live in that section."

In the newspaper the other day, I read how Palmer C. Hayden, a Negro, 33 years old, was quitting his scrub bucket to study art in Europe. He had just won the $400 prize in art awarded by the Harmon Foundation. He had the courage to start something.

I know a young fellow who, while still in College, got the idea through a chance occurrence that there was an entirely virgin field among the undertakers for raincoats—black raincoats. He reasoned that there were so few undertakers in each city that no store could afford to carry a complete range of sizes for them, whereas one central store, selling to the whole country, could do so.

So he borrowed a few dollars and tried out his idea by mail. Today he is a millionaire—and it has all been the logical outcome of that one idea.

He started something.

If you could only realize that you have a definite place in a scheme so big that God has been working millions of years to bring it about; if you would only remember that every forward step you take has His approval and help; if you would look upon Him as a

Chapter 5: Start Something!

loving Father watching you, His little son, taking a few faltering steps, ready to catch you when you stumble, ready to help you over the difficult places, ready to strengthen and support you—how much of fear and worry you would avoid, how much more surely you would progress.

"If ye walk in my statutes, and keep my commandments, and do them;

"Then I will give you rain in due season, and the land shall yield her increase, and the trees of the field shall yield their fruit.

"And your threshing shall reach unto the vintage, and the vintage shall reach unto the sowing time: and ye shall eat your bread to the full, and dwell in your land safely.

"And I will give peace in the land, and ye shall lie down, and none shall make you afraid."—Leviticus 26:3-6.

But to progress, it is necessary that you learn to take a few steps for yourself. You can't remain tied to the Father's apron-strings if you are to become a man or woman worthy of the name.

You know how much these "Mother's darlings" are good for when they get out among other boys. You know how long these pampered children of the rich usually last, when they are thrown upon their own resources.

The Father above has the wisdom and the courage to do what very few earthly fathers can. He gives his children free will. He turns them loose, in a world full of pitfalls and dangers, to learn self-reliance, to become real men and women, worthy Sons of God.

Yet He is always just behind us. His arms ready to support us. His hand to guide us. His wisdom to counsel us—if only we will realize His presence. His solicitude, His Fatherly love and care.

Chapter 5: Start Something!

"He giveth power to the faint; and to them that have no might, he increaseth strength."—Isaiah 40:29.

He has given us free will, so He will not force Himself upon us. He has untied our apron-strings, so He won't *make* us take the great place He plans for us in the Divine scheme of things. But if we will learn to work with Him, if we will treat Him as a Father, run to Him with our joys as with our sorrows, have Him at the back of all our plans, know that we can rely upon His help in all our undertakings, what a difference it will make!

You need never hesitate, then, to start anything of good, because you will know that with Him behind you, it can not fail. You will never lack the faith, the enthusiasm, the power to carry through even the most difficult undertaking. Most of all, you will never lack the will to begin, for you will know that even the Father can not help you to accomplish until you yourself have taken the first step by STARTING SOMETHING!

"Since receiving your first books," writes M. D. C. of Capitola, California, "I have made, from insurance premiums in a new company which I was instrumental in forming, more than $100,000.00 in a little over six months' time. My previous income over a period of years has been approximately $7,500.00 per year."

He started something!

The Starting Point

Now, how about you—have *you* started anything? Do you want to? Then let's take stock of you for a moment:

1. The first thing to do is to list all of your successes, no matter how unimportant they may seem. Go back to your boyhood days. What was your favorite game? Was it one that required initiative, quick

Chapter 5: Start Something!

thinking, prompt action? Were you a better "individual player" or "team-player"? In other words, were you a brilliant "star," or one of those who could sink his own individuality for the good of the team?

Did you ever captain any team successfully? Did your teammates like you, work with you enthusiastically? Could you inspire loyalty, cooperation, weld your team into a single unit with a common purpose?

Qualities such as these can be acquired, of course, but if you had them naturally as a boy, then you have them now, so by all means develop them to their fullest extent. They can be made your most valuable assets in business.

2. What sort of game do you prefer now? One that depends primarily upon yourself— or one that demands mostly teamwork? Games are wonderful indicators, you know, of your innate characteristics. I used to know a very shrewd old fellow who never formed a business friendship until after he had played poker with his prospective friend. How do you play bridge—with your partner or regardless of him? How do you play tennis—as two individual players, or as a team?

Don't misunderstand me—I am not decrying brilliant individual play. I am just trying to get you to analyze your innate characteristics. If you play best alone, by all means concentrate on the kind of work or the kind of business that is built up around one single figure. On the other hand, if your forte is teamwork, cooperation —go in for organized effort where your leadership and fairness and good-fellowship will have the greatest play.

3. List your characteristics frankly. Ability in particular lines, quickness in picking up new ideas, open-mindedness, versatility, honesty, sociability, interest in others, power to convince others, courage, aggressiveness, stick-to-it-iveness.

Chapter 5: Start Something!

In short, analyze yourself frankly—then from that analysis, from your past failures and successes, pick the work you have the greatest aptitude for—and go into it!

Don't go into it blindly. First study it. There are good books on every phase of business today. There are correspondence courses as good as any taught in colleges. Get them. Read them. Set your goal. Make your plans carefully. Start them in a small way first. Test each step before you put your weight upon it. But once sure of it, put your whole weight into it—your money and your ability and all your thought— *particularly all your thought.*

Don't scatter your energies. You can do it with the work of your hands but you can't do it with your thought. To make a great success, your thought has to be concentrated on your goal in the same way that the Marconi beam system concentrates all the power of its rays in the one direction. "No man can serve two masters"—with justice to either.

Choose your goal; then, like the searchlight, concentrate all your efforts, all your energies, all your thoughts in the one direction. Don't go running off after false gods. Don't fritter away your energies on inconsequential side issues. Focus them—focus them as you focus the rays of the sun through a magnifying glass. Do that—and you will speedily start something!

There is a definite place for you in the Divine plan. There is a work which you are to do, which no one else can do quite as well. Pray, therefore, to the Father that He may open your eyes to your right work, that He may open your ears to the promptings of His voice, that He may open your understanding of the right way.

"I will instruct thee and teach thee in the way which thou shall go: I will guide thee with mine eye."—Psalms 32;8.

Chapter 6: Rough Diamonds

OVER in the northwestern corner of Pennsylvania a few years ago, there lived a farmer who was interested in oil. His brother was in the oil business in Canada and had told him that fortunes were being made in it every day. So he sent for all kinds of books that told how and where to locate oil, took a course in geology, spent two years getting ready—and then sold his farm and went to Canada to work in the oil fields.

The man who bought the farm, walking over the place next morning, came to a little brook that ran through the middle of it. There was a heavy board across the brook to hold back the surface drift, and back of it for some yards the water was coated with a thick scum.

It seems that this scum had troubled the previous owner for a long time. The cattle wouldn't drink the water with it on it. So he had conceived the idea of the board to clear the scum from the surface and let the cattle drink from the water below.

To the new buyer, that "scum" looked and smelled and tasted suspiciously like oil! He sent for experts. They bored. And opened up one of the richest oil fields in Pennsylvania!

It is natural to think that the first step towards success is to go somewhere else or into some new business. The distant pastures always look greenest. But more often than not, our best opportunities lie right under our own nose.

When the original Pennsylvania oil wells seemed to be worked out, most of the oil men set off for fields and pastures new. But a few stayed. And those few found that the surface had merely been scratched! Instead of being worked out, scarcely 15 percent of the oil had been taken out of the ground. By the pressure system, or by

Chapter 6: Rough Diamonds

boring deeper and striking new deposits, they found the other 85 percent!

And that is only one industry out of hundreds where fortunes have been made out of what other men had thrown away as worthless. No one has yet exhausted any line of thought. The inventions that mankind has already made are merely the introduction to bigger and greater things—the open door to opportunity. The most brilliant scientists are the first to tell you that their discoveries are but as a drop of water to the great ocean of achievement that lies beyond.

"For the earth shall be filled with the knowledge of the glory of the Lord, as the waters cover the sea."—Habakuk 2:14.

Nearly a century and a half ago, Malthus propounded his famous theory that population, when unchecked, tends to increase in geometrical proportion, whereas subsistence increases only in arithmetical proportion. In other words, that population increases many times as rapidly as the means of subsistence. And he visioned a time in the very near future when artificial checks would have to be put on population, or the world would starve.

Population has increased very near to the point he feared, but what has happened? We are farther away from the saturation point than in his day! The age of machinery came along; the age of scientific experiment; and these not only opened up new fields through better transportation, but greatly increased the yields in present fields. Now Prof. Albrecht Penck advances the belief that by the year 2227 there will be 8,000,000,000 people here on earth—and famine will be continuous, because the earth cannot support that many!

What little faith some of these economists have! They get so wrapped up in their own calculations that they can see nothing else. "By that time (2227 A. D.)," says the New York *Herald Tribune,* "man may be taking foodstuffs from the sunlight, from the air or

Chapter 6: Rough Diamonds

from the power of the revolving earth! The only safe prediction about the future of man is that no limit dare be set to what he and Nature may cooperate to do."

"For I know the thoughts that I think towards you, saith the Lord, thoughts of peace and not of evil, to give you an expected end. Then, shall ye call upon me, and ye shall go and pray unto me and I will hearken unto you. And ye shall seek me, and find me, when ye shall search for me with all your heart."— Jeremiah 29:11-13.

For 5,000 years men have built houses of brick, and in all of that time there had been no change made, either in the tools used, or in the manner in which the work was done.

Along came Frank Gilbreth, studied the motions involved in laying brick, reduced them from eighteen to five, and increased the hourly output from 120 to 350 bricks!

Simple enough—but it took 5,000 years for someone to think up this simple solution. For 5,000 years mankind has been taught that some men are born with ability—some without—and that those without must serve those who have it.

No greater mistake was ever made. Every man is born with ability sufficient to carry him upward to the highest rung of success. "Ordinary ability, properly applied," said Theodore N. Vail, "is all that is necessary to reach the highest rung in the ladder of success."

Life's biggest blunder is to underestimate your own power to develop and accomplish. What if you are handicapped by lack of education, by poverty, by self-consciousness, by sickness, by some physical disability?

Thank God for it! A handicap is the greatest urge you can have towards success. Like the eagle which uses adverse winds to rise higher, you can mount to success on your handicap.

Chapter 6: Rough Diamonds

In an editorial some time ago, the *New York Globe* observed: "Nature is not democratic. She gives some women beauty and leaves others, of equal or greater merit, plain. She makes some persons intelligent and some stupid. In brief, we are not born free and equal nor do we become so. To some the Gods bring gifts and others they pass by. There are aristocracies of voices, of beauty and of intelligence. The best that democracy can ever do is to give every Caruso a chance to sing."

That is the general belief. That is the idea that prevails among most casual thinkers. But the man who thinks thus is overlooking the greatest force in life— the reserve force that lies so dormant in most of us—the power of the Spirit within to rise superior to any inequality, to overcome any seeming handicap or difficulty.

The greatest thing that can happen to any man is the discovery of this all-powerful Spirit within him. If it is necessary for him to undergo hunger, if it is necessary for him to suffer sickness or injury in order to make the discovery, let him suffer it cheerfully, gladly! No price is too high to pay to bring into your affairs the power of the Holy Spirit. For everything you have suffered, everything you have paid, will be made good to you a hundredfold. There is no maybe about this. I have seen it work out hundreds of times. I have learned it from very bitter experience. As in the case of Job of olden times:

"The Lord gave Job twice as much as he had before.

"So the Lord blessed the latter end of Job more than his beginning; for he had fourteen thousand sheep, and six thousand camels, and a thousand yoke of oxen and a thousand she asses.

"He had also seven sons and three daughters."—Job 42:10, 12, 13.

The Law of Compensation

Chapter 6: Rough Diamonds

What was it made Demosthenes the greatest orator of all time? NOT his natural gifts—but his natural handicaps! He was self-conscious. And he stuttered. Had he not been thus handicapped, he would probably have become a mediocre orator—and lived and died unknown to the world. But he had to study so hard to overcome his natural handicaps, he had to practice and work so long and so whole-heartedly, that when at last he was ready to appear before the public, his conscious efforts were backed by all the powers of the subconscious. He had so often called upon the Spirit within to help him in his practice that it came to his aid of Itself when the real need arose. It stood at his back to give him confidence, to lend him inspiration, to supply the power that moved his hearers as they had never been moved before.

In "Organ Inferiority and Its Psychic Compensation," Dr. Adler brings out the well-known scientific fact that any physical weakness or inferiority brings with it an extra urge to strive for superiority in some compensating way.

Napoleon, Caesar, Prince Eugene were little men, but the urge within them made them the biggest men of their day.

Whistler, the greater painter, had poor eyes. He was said to be colorblind. So he became a master in nuances. Edison was deaf—so he perfected the talking machine.

Beethoven, Mozart, Franz—all had defects in hearing. And worked so hard at their music that they became masters of technique, and musical geniuses.

The same principle applies to nations. Take Alaska and Switzerland as an instance. Alaska has enormous resources of gold and silver and copper and coal, vast virgin forests, 1,000,000 square miles suitable for agriculture, and the greatest fisheries in the world. Yet if Alaska were as densely populated as Switzerland it would be

Chapter 6: Rough Diamonds

supporting 120,000,000 inhabitants!

The Swiss have few natural resources, so they are constrained to use their ingenuity instead. They take a ton of metal and put it together in such form as to make it worth a million dollars. They take cotton thread at 20 cents a pound, and convert it into lace worth $2,000 a pound. They take a block of wood worth 10 cents and convert it into a carving worth $100. And because as a nation they have learned the art of utilizing their talents, they have prospered abundantly.

Where is the moral? Simply this:

There is no lack, no handicap, *nothing,* that can defeat you. Obstacles are the greatest blessings God can give you. They bring out the soul of you. They bring the Holy Spirit to your help. And anything which acquaints you with the Spirit within you, anything that gives you an understanding of the infinite power within you, anything that brings the Holy Spirit into your daily affairs, is worthwhile no matter what its cost.

"And Jacob was left alone; and there wrestled a man with him until the breaking of the day.

"And when he saw that he prevailed not against him, he touched the hollow of his thigh; and the hollow of Jacob's thigh was out of joint, as he wrestled with him.

"And he said, Let me go, for the day breaketh. And he said, I will not let thee go, *except thou bless me.*

"And he said unto him, What is thy name? And he said, Jacob.

"And he said,, Thy name shall be called no more Jacob, but Israel: for as a prince hast thou power with God and with men, and hast prevailed.

Chapter 6: Rough Diamonds

"And Jacob asked him, and said, Tell me, I pray thee, thy name. And he said, Wherefore is it that thou dost ask after my name? *And he blessed him there.*"

That is what you, too, must do. Wrestle with every difficulty until you have learned something from it. Don't let go of any trouble until you have made it bless you.

Remember that back of you always is the power of the Holy Spirit and if the need arises, it can give you the strength—not merely of one man, but of ten! Like David going out to meet Goliath, realize that it is not you who is fighting the battle, but God. "Be not afraid, nor dismayed by reason of this great multitude; for the battle is not yours but God's."—II Chronicles 20:15. Knowing that, no obstacle need deter you, no experience terrify you. With God on your side, you are always in the majority. Struggles and trials are mere growing pains of your soul, to teach you that, though terrifying to you alone, they are as nothing to you when allied to the Father through the Holy Spirit.

Before you give up where you are and move to distant fields, before you seek your fortune afar, look around you! See if some of the riches in your own back yard won't bear cultivating.

There is a story told of an old Boer farmer living on a rocky bit of ground on the road between Kimberley and Pretoria. Scattered here and there over the ground, they often found dull looking pieces of crystal. The boys used them to throw at the sheep. Until one day a Cecil Rhodes engineer happened that way—*and discovered them to be diamonds!*

Many of us are just as literally walking on diamonds in the rough as were that farmer's boys. Only most of us never know it until someone comes along and points them out to us.

Chapter 6: Rough Diamonds

Let us resolve to do some of this discovering for our own selves. Let us look at every job with the question—how can this be done easier, quicker, better? Let us devote part of our thoughts to finding new outlets, new methods, new needs. Let us get a fixed objective—and then work towards it. Some great thinker once said that we should be a world of successes if the idea of a fixed objective and a set goal possessed us.

A fixed objective—it serves much the same as the controlling idea outlined in Chapter 3, magnetizing your thoughts and your work and yourself with the one intense desire. Add to that a sublime faith that shall bring the Holy Spirit within into cooperation with you—and your objective is assured.

"First have something good," said Horace Greeley, "then advertise!" First have your fixed objective, then call upon the Holy Spirit to help you, and there is no goal you cannot win.

"For the vision is yet for an appointed time, but at the end it shall speak, and not lie; though it tarry, wait for it; because it will surely come; it will not tarry."— Habakkuk 2:3.

I know a man who had a $2,500 job. He had just been offered another paying $500 more. And he went to a friend of mine to ask his advice about changing. The first question my friend asked was what he had to offer these new people. He told him, the usual round of routine knowledge.

"That isn't worth much," my friend informed him. "These people are in the same line of business that you have been working at for years. If in all those years you haven't thought out ways in which that work could be vastly improved, if you haven't been perfecting in your own mind short cuts, money-saving ways, practical ideas—then hold on to your $2,500 job until you do. You're not worth a cent more.

Chapter 6: Rough Diamonds

"My advice to you is to go home and write down on paper what you have to offer this new firm. What new methods you can show them that any other $2,500 man can't. What new ideas you have that will make money for them.

"When you get them all down, center your attention on the best of them, and work it out. Then go to these people and tell them you will give them your idea and your services—NOT for $3,000, but for $6,000!"

That talk woke this man up. He did some really serious thinking for the first time in his business life. With the result that he refused the $3,000 offer then, but kept the position open for a few weeks until he could get his big idea ready.

Then he not only landed his $6,000 but made good on his idea so completely that within six months that $6,000 was increased to $7,200.

"There is guidance for each one of us," says Emerson, "and by lowly listening we shall hear the right word." Give of your best—not merely in manual labor but in ideas—and you can safely leave the rest to the guidance of the Holy Spirit within.

As pointed out in *The Secret of the Ages,* the basic principles of all business are the same, be they as big as the Steel Trust or as small as the corner newsstand. The whole practice of commerce is founded upon them. Summed up, and boiled down to the fewest possible words, they are two:

1—Give to get.

2—This one thing I do.

1—You can get away with dishonest values, with poor service, for a little while. You can take two dollars worth of value for every one

Chapter 6: Rough Diamonds

you give. But the Law of Karma will get you soon or late. If you intend to stay in business, it pays to make it a rule to try to give a little more of value or of service than you are paid for.

2—Remember that each task, no matter how great, is but a group of little tasks, any one of which you can easily do. Like the great New York subways, it is but a succession of cellars connected together. Find a place to start. Take the first step. The rest will follow easily.

So many are afraid of giving too much for the amount that is paid them. And so many wives get inflated ideas of their husband's value to or work in a business, and urge them not to give so much unless the business pays them more for it.

Poor things—they mean well. But no man ever has to be urged not to work too hard at his business. He can work too hard at worrying about it—yes. But every bit of honest work he puts into his business will pay him an honest return. He is not working merely for some man or some institution. He is doing God's work. And God is the most generous Paymaster there is. He doesn't label His paychecks. He doesn't say—"This is in payment of such-and-such invoices." But the pay comes—just as surely as the day follows night.

"I cause those that love me to inherit substance; and I will fill their treasures."— Proverbs 8:21.

There is a place for you in the Divine plan—a place that no one but you can fill. There is a work for you in the great scheme of things —a work that no one can do as well as you.

So, if you have been drifting, if your work has been joyless, your business profitless, look around you for the right niche that was made for you to fill. Don't mind how humble it may seem. To do even the most humble thing supremely well is artistry—and will bring its reward. Let your daily prayer to the Spirit within you be

Chapter 6: Rough Diamonds

that He manifest the Divine design in your life—that He bring you to your proper work, your right place.

Say to Him each day, as F. S. Shinn suggests in *The Game of Life and How to Play It*—"Infinite Spirit, open the way for the Divine design in my life to manifest. Let the genius within me now be released. Let me see clearly the perfect plan."

And then, if you like, ask Him to give you a lead, an indication of the next step for you to take.

"Call upon the Almighty," says the old Eastern Sage. "He will help thee. Thou needst not perplex thyself about anything else. Shut thy eyes and while thou art asleep, God will change thy bad fortune into good."

"Blessed is the man that trusteth in the Lord, and whose hope the Lord is. For he shall be as a tree planted by the waters, and that spreadeth out her roots by the river, and shall not see when heat cometh, but her leaf shall be green; and shall not be careful in the year of drought, neither shall cease from yielding fruit."—JEREMIAH 17:7-8.

Chapter 7: Ich Dien—I Serve

YOU want riches. You want five talents, ten talents, a thousand—a million. But what have you to offer in return? Has it never occurred to you that you must make an accounting of them?

If someone were to offer you a million right now, what would you do with it? Buy a yacht—an automobile—have a good time! But what sort of an accounting would that make for the Master? And why should He put Himself out to place riches in hands no better prepared to use them to good purpose than that?

Suppose you went to a banker for money—a banker who knew you well—and asked him to lend you $100,000. What is the first question he would ask of you? "What are you going to do with it?"

If you could give him no better answer than—"Buy a yacht, an automobile, have a good time"—how much do you suppose he would lend you? Not a red cent! No more will the Father which is in Heaven.

You have got to have an idea first before you can borrow money from a bank. And if the banker is wise, he will make you prove your idea in a small way before he will advance you any great sum to spend upon it.

And when you approach the Father for ten talents or a thousand, you must first have an idea that will be of some benefit to mankind.

Henry Ford is worth a billion dollars. He is probably the richest man in the world. How did he get it?

He started out with an idea—an idea that the automobile should be put within reach of everyone. That idea was of definite benefit to mankind. It opened up remote districts. It brought light and life into

Chapter 7: Ich Dien—I Serve

the lives of millions of farm dwellers. He was entitled to a generous reward.

Woolworth accumulated a fortune of millions. He performed a definite service. So did Penny. So has many another merchant on a smaller scale. And the supply flows to him in proportion. But before reward, must come the idea. You must give to get.

The United States has become the richest of all peoples. Half the world's gold is in our possession. In 75 years the wealth of the country has increased fifty times over. All the world has become richer, but in no other country has the wealth increased to anything like that extent. Why?

Some will say because of our great natural resources. But Mexico has great natural resources. So has Russia. And China. Yet all these countries are backward.

What then is the answer?

The fact that in America manufacturers have learned to share with the workers the fruits of industry. America began to forge ahead of the rest of the world the moment its manufacturers learned that every worker was entitled to a share of the good things of life.

Automobile manufacturers saw every workman as a potential automobile owner. And then proceeded to make that ideal feasible. Telephone companies, gas companies, electric light and equipment companies, radio manufacturers, saw every home as a user of their products—and proceeded to put them within the reach of all.

Never since life first appeared upon this planet has there been so much of comfort, happiness and contentment among all the people as there is in these United States. And the reason? Free education. Equal opportunity. And the realization on the part of manufacturers that their best market and their biggest one is right among the

Chapter 7: Ich Dien—I Serve

workers—that the more they share with the workers, the more will come back to them.

You must give to get.

Russia has enormous resources of land and minerals and oil. So has China. And Mexico.
Why then are they so poor?

Because the ruling classes have tried to keep all these riches for themselves. They wanted to take all—and give nothing. That may work for a little while, but always there is an accounting.

"For they have sown the wind, and they shall reap the whirlwind: it hath no stalk: the bud shall yield no meal: if so be it yield, the strangers shall swallow it up."—Hosea 8:7.

You must give to get.

There is a story by Samuel Butler that describes the idea exactly:

"In Erehwon," he says, "he who makes a colossal fortune in the hosiery trade and by his energy has succeeded in reducing the price of woolen goods by the thousandeth part of a penny in a pound, this man is worth ten professional philanthropists. So strongly are the Erehwonians impressed with this that if a man has made a fortune of over £20,000 a year they exempt him from all taxation, considering him as a work of art and too precious to be meddled with. They say, 'How much he must have done for society before society could be prevailed upon to give him so much money!' "

Unfortunately, we have not yet reached the ideal state visioned by Butler, where every millionaire earned his money through unusual service to the community. Too many are still robber captains or greedy moneylenders like Cassim.

Chapter 7: Ich Dien—I Serve

The Law of Karma is steadily at work. Give it time. There is always an accounting. Meantime, thank God for the Fords and the Edisons and the Burbanks and the thousands of others of their kind who are not only making this the richest country on earth, but are helping to spread those riches around and make it also the happiest.

The Bank of God

The true purpose of every worthy business is to help in the distribution of God's gifts among men.

Judge your work, your ideas, by that standard. If you want money, if you seek riches, ask yourself—"Could I go to God and tell Him as my banker that the purpose for which I want this money is anything but a selfish one? Could I honestly assure Him that my primary idea is service—giving to people a little better value, a little more of service, a little greater comfort or convenience or happiness than they are now getting?"

Don't misunderstand me. You are entitled to money to meet your daily needs. You have a right to ask for all those things necessary to your happiness, as long as they do not infringe upon the happiness of others. You even have a right to demand just as much more than that as you can use to advantage. But you have got to account for it!

Given a right idea, given a controlling thought, dollars will seek you, even as iron filings seek the magnet. You can claim all that you can use to good advantage.

So get your thought right first. Make sure that you have something the world needs. Then draw on the Great Banker for all the money you need, never fearing, never doubting that He will honor your draft.

"For the Lord God is a sun and shield. The Lord will give grace and glory. No good thing will he withhold from them that walk

Chapter 7: Ich Dien—I Serve

uprightly."—Psalms 84:11.

After all the proofs of God's power to supply them with food and water; after He had brought them safely through every conceivable danger; when another crucial time came, the children of Israel fearfully called out—"Can God furnish us a table in the wilderness?"— Psalms 78:19.

Of course He can!

"Hast thou not known? Hast thou not heard? That the everlasting God, the Lord, the Creator of the ends of the earth, fainteth not, neither is weary?"—Isaiah 40:28.

Draw on Him as you need. Don't wait to start until you have all the money in hand. How many businesses—big and successful today—do you suppose would have been started if their founders had waited until they had all the money in hand they were going to need? Use the talent you have. Your credit is good for just as much more as you can use to advantage. More than that is a weight around your neck.

If you had a business proposition, and knew that your banker would extend you credit to the extent of a million dollars to develop it, you wouldn't think of drawing that million all at once. No—you would ask for credit as you needed it. You would draw upon it only as your business required it. You wouldn't burden yourself with one cent more of interest than was necessary.

Do likewise with the Lord. If your banker promised you the money as you needed it, you would go ahead with your plans, secure in the knowledge that his word was just as good as the actual money in the bank. Do you rate the promises of the Father any lower than those of man?

Chapter 7: Ich Dien—I Serve

"Be glad then, ye children of Zion, and rejoice in the Lord your God: for he hath given you the former rain moderately, and he will cause to come down for you the rain, the former rain, and the latter rain in the first month.

"And the floors shall be full of wheat, and the vats shall overflow with wine and oil.

"And ye shall eat in plenty, and be satisfied, and praise the name of the Lord your God, that hath dealt wondrously with you: and my people shall never be ashamed.

"And ye shall know that I am in the midst of Israel, and that I am the Lord your God, and none else: and my people shall never be ashamed."—JOEL 2:21, 23, 24, 26, 27.

What is it you want money for? Get your idea clearly in mind. Satisfy yourself that it is for a worthy purpose. And when you are thoroughly satisfied of that, then go right ahead with your plans.

How much do you need for this stage of them? How much would you draw on the bank for, this moment, if you had unlimited credit there? $100? $1,000? $10,000? Explain your need to the Father just as you would to a very wise and sympathetic banker. Then tell Him you are drawing upon Him for that amount. Actually write out a draft and mail it—anywhere—to me if you like. Then go about your plans as confidently, as believingly, as though the Father's Bank were just around the corner.

But don't try to fool yourself. Above all, don't try to deceive the Father. Don't camouflage merely selfish desires in some high and mighty guise as benefits to mankind.

Remember the old Spanish Conquistadores? Freebooters they were—neither more nor less—searching for booty, and caring not how

Chapter 7: Ich Dien—I Serve

they came by it. They robbed the Indians, they massacred thousands, they enslaved whole nations—all for lust of gold.

But that wasn't their tale about it. They put it all upon the high and mighty plane of spreading Christianity, of saving the souls of the heathen.

It worked for the Spaniards for a little while. But they became so puffed up that they thought to use the same ideas upon the heretics of England, of the Netherlands, upon the entire world. Then came the disastrous Armada, followed by swift and certain decline.

It was only 300 years ago that Spain was the richest nation in the world, her power pre-eminent in Europe, her sovereignty extending over most of America. Now look at her—even the Riffians laughed at her until France came to her aid.

We reap what we sow. A grain of corn planted reproduces only corn. A grain of wheat brings forth wheat. And the seed of the deadly nightshade brings forth poisonous flowers.

God cannot be mocked. We reap in kind exactly as we sow.

What then shall you do to succeed? What is the modern law of business? The same as two commandments given to us thousands of years ago:

"Thou shalt love the Lord thy God with all thy heart and with all thy soul and with all thy mind." And, "Thou shalt love thy neighbor as thyself."

"Thou shalt love the Lord thy God." Thou shalt use the talents He has given thee. Thou shalt use them to benefit thy neighbor, to benefit all of mankind, and in so doing thou shalt benefit thyself. Do that, and thy Lord will say unto thee: "Well done, thou good and faithful servant; thou hast been faithful over a few things, I will make thee ruler over many things: enter thou into the joy of thy Lord."

But to those who fail to use, or who abuse their talent, the Lord says even as he did of the unprofitable servant: "Take therefore the talent from him and cast him into outer darkness: there shall be weeping and gnashing of teeth."

Chapter 8: The Coming of the Spirit

THERE was a certain Sultan of the Indies that had three sons, the eldest called Houssain, the second Ali, the third Ahmed.

He had also a niece, remarkable for her wit and beauty, named Nouronnihar, whom all three Princes loved and desired to wed.

Their father remonstrated with them, pointed out the troubles that would ensue if they persisted in their attachment, and did all he could to persuade them to abide by his choice of which of them should wed her.

Failing that, he sent for them one day and suggested that the three Princes should depart on a three-months' journey, each to a different country. Upon their return, whichever one should bring to him the most extraordinary rarity as a gift, should receive the Princess in marriage.

The three Princes cheerfully consented to this, each flattering himself that fortune would prove favorable to him. The Sultan gave them money, and early next morning they all went out at the same gate of the city, each dressed like a merchant, attended by a trusty officer habited as a slave, and all well mounted and equipped. The first day's journey they proceeded together; and at night, when they were at supper, they agreed to meet again in three months at the khan where they were stopping; and that the first who came should wait for the rest; so that as they had all three taken leave together of the Sultan, they might return in company. The next morning, after they had embraced and wished each other success, they mounted their horses, and took each a different road.

Prince Houssain, the eldest brother, had heard of the riches and splendor of the kingdom of Bisnagar and bent his course toward it.

Chapter 8: The Coming of the Spirit

Arriving there, he betook himself to the quarters of the traders, where a merchant, seeing him go by much fatigued, invited him to sit down in front of his shop. He had not been seated long before a crier appeared, with a small piece of carpeting on his arm, for which he asked forty purses. The Prince told him that he could not understand how so small a piece of carpeting could be set at so high a price, unless it had something very extraordinary about it which failed to show in its appearance.

You have guessed right, sir," I replied the crier; "whoever sits on this piece of carpeting may be carried in an instant wherever he desires." "If that is so," said the Prince, "I shall not think forty purses too much." "Sir," replied the crier, "I have told you the truth. Let us go into the back warehouse, where I will spread the carpet. When we have both sat down, form the wish to be transported into your apartment at the khan, and if we are not conveyed there at once, it shall be no bargain."

On the Prince agreeing to this, they went into the merchant's back shop, where they both sat down on the carpet; and as soon as the Prince had expressed his wish to be carried to his apartment at the khan, he in an instant found himself and the crier there. After this convincing proof of the virtue of the carpet, he paid over to the crier forty purses of gold, together with an extra purse for himself.

Prince Houssain was overjoyed at his good fortune, never doubting that this rare carpet would gain him the possession of the beautiful Nouronnihar.

After seeing all the wonders of Bisnagar, Prince Houssain wished to be nearer his dear Princess, so he took and spread the carpet, and with the officer whom he had brought with him, commanded the carpet to transport them to the caravansery at which he and his brothers were to meet, where he passed for a merchant till their arrival.

Chapter 8: The Coming of the Spirit

Prince Ali, the second brother, designed to travel into Persia, so, after parting with his brothers, joined a caravan, and soon arrived at Shiraz, the capital of that empire.

Walking through the quarters of the jewelers, he was not a little surprised to see one who held in his hand an ivory tube, about a foot in length, and about an inch thick, which he priced at fifty purses. At first he thought the man mad, and asked him what he meant by asking fifty purses for a tube which seemed scarcely worth one. The jeweler replied, "Sir, you shall judge yourself whether I am mad or not, when I have told you the property of this tube. By looking through it, you can see whatever object you wish to behold."

The jeweler presented the tube to the Prince, and he looked through it, wishing at the same time to see the Sultan his father. Immediately he saw before him the image of his father, sitting on his throne, in the midst of his council. Next, he wished to see the Princess Nouronnihar; and instantly beheld her laughing and talking with the women about her.

Prince Ali needed no other proof to persuade him that this tube was the most valuable of gifts in all the world, and taking the crier to the khan where he lodged, paid him his fifty purses and received the tube.

Prince Ali was overjoyed at his purchase, for he felt fully assured that his brothers would not be able to meet with anything so rare and admirable, and the Princess Nouronnihar would be his. His only thought now was to get back to the rendezvous as speedily as might be, so without waiting to visit any of the wonders of Shiraz, he joined a party of merchants and arrived without accident at the place appointed, where he found Prince Houssain, and both waited for Prince Ahmed.

Prince Ahmed had taken the road to Samarcand, and the day after

Chapter 8: The Coming of the Spirit

his arrival went, as his brothers had done, into the merchants quarters, where he had not walked long before he heard a crier, with an artificial apple in his hand, offer it at five-and-forty purses. "Let me see your apple," he said to the man, "and tell me what extraordinary property it possesses, to be valued at so high a rate." "Sir," replied the crier, giving the apple into his hand, "if you look at the mere outside of this apple it is not very remarkable; but if you consider its miraculous properties, you will say it is invaluable. It cures sick people of every manner of disease. Even if a person is dying, it will cure him instantly, and this merely by his smelling of the apple."

"If that be true," replied Prince Ahmed, "this apple is indeed invaluable; but how am I to know that it is true?'" "Sir," replied the crier, "the truth is attested by the whole city of Samarcand; ask any of these merchants here. Several of them will tell you they had not been alive today had it not been for this excellent remedy."

Many people had gathered round while they talked, and now confirmed what the crier had declared. One among them said he had a friend dangerously ill, whose life was despaired of; so they could now see for themselves the truth of all that was said. Upon this Prince Ahmed told the crier he would give him forty-five purses for the apple if it cured the sick person by smelling it.

"Come, sir," said the crier to Prince Ahmed, "let us go and do it, and the apple shall be yours."

The sick man smelled of the apple, and was cured; and the prince, after he had paid the forty-five purses, received the apple. He then joined himself to the first caravan that set out for the Indies, and arrived in perfect health at the caravansery, where the Princes Houssain and Ali waited for him.

The brothers embraced with tenderness, and felicitated each other on their safe journeys.

Chapter 8: The Coming of the Spirit

They then fell to comparing gifts. Houssain showed the carpet and told how it had brought him thither. Ali brought out the ivory tube, and nothing would do but they must at once look through it at their beloved. But—alas and alack! For the sight that met their eyes. The Princess Nouronnihar lay stretched on her bed, seemingly at the point of death.

When Prince Ahmed had seen this, he turned to his two brothers. "Make haste," he adjured them, "lose no time; we may save her life. This apple which I hold here has this wonderful property—its smell will restore to life a sick person. I have tried it and will show you its wonderful effect on the Princess, if you will but hasten to her."

"If haste be all," answered Houssain, "we cannot do better than transport ourselves instantly into her chamber on my magic carpet. Come, lose no time, sit down, it is large enough to hold us all."

The order was no sooner given than they found themselves carried into the Princess Nouronnihar's chamber.

Prince Ahmed rose off the carpet, and went to her bedside, where he put the apple to her nostrils. Immediately the Princess opened her eyes, expressed her joy at seeing them, and thanked them all for their efforts in her behalf.

While she was dressing, the Princes went to present themselves to the Sultan, their father. The Sultan received them with joy. The Princes presented each the rarity which he had brought, and begged of him to pronounce their fate.

The Sultan of the Indies considered what answer he should make. At last he said, "I would that I could declare for one of you, my sons, but I cannot do it with justice. It is true, Ahmed, that the Princess owes her cure to your artificial apple; but let me ask you, could you have cured her if you had not known of the danger she

Chapter 8: The Coming of the Spirit

was in through Ali's tube, and if Houssain's carpet had not brought you to her so quickly? Your tube, Ali, discovered to you and your brothers the illness of your cousin; but the knowledge of her illness would have been of no service without the artificial apple and the carpet. And as for you, Houssain, your carpet was an essential instrument in effecting her cure. But it would have been of little use, if you had not known of her illness through All's tube, or if Ahmed had not been there with his artificial apple. Therefore, as I see it, the carpet, the ivory tube, and the artificial apple have no preference over each other, on the contrary, each had an equal share in her cure."

The story goes on to tell how the Sultan, after repeated trials, finally did choose a husband for the Princess. How Prince Ali wed her. How Prince Ahmed wandered away, disconsolate. How he met the Fairy Princess Banou. And how through her he finally won the greatest prize of all—contact with the Spirit within that knows all, sees all and can do all things.

In *The Secret of the Ages,* I endeavored to show how your subconscious mind can be made to serve as the Ivory Tube, giving you the answer to any problem you may put up to it in the right way.

In later volumes of this set, I shall try to prove to you how the Spirit within can and gladly will serve you better than Magic Carpet or Curative Apple. Length of days is in His right hand, freedom from fear, protection from harm, health, happiness and prosperity.

Do I promise too much? Just listen:

"But be ye glad and rejoice for ever in that which I create: for, behold, I create Jerusalem a rejoicing, and her people a joy.

"And I will rejoice in Jerusalem, and joy in my people: and the voice of weeping shall be no more heard in her, nor the voice of

Chapter 8: The Coming of the Spirit

crying.

"There shall be no more thence an infant of days, nor an old man that hath not filled his days:

"And they shall build houses, and inhabit them; and they shall plant vineyards, and eat the fruit of them.

"They shall not build, and another inhabit; they shall not plant, and another eat: for as the days of a tree are the days of my people, and mine elect shall long enjoy the work of their hands.

"They shall not labour in vain, nor bring forth for trouble; for they are the seed of the blessed of the Lord, and their offspring with them.

"And it shall come to pass, that before they call, I will answer; and while they are yet speaking, I will hear."—ISAIAH 65:18-24.

But how to find this Kingdom? How shall we bring the Holy Spirit into our lives?

By going into the quiet, into thought. By concentrating all thoughts on communing with the Father above, without outside distractions. By praying. And if we will pray rightly, the heaven will open to us and God will come upon us.

But He will never do it for the mere repetition of lip prayers that we have learned by rote.

The Soul's Sincere Desire

Do you know what prayer is? Just an earnest desire that we take to God—to Universal Mind—for fulfillment. As Montgomery puts it —"Prayer is the soul's sincere desire, uttered or unexpressed." It is our Heart's Desire. At least, the only prayer that is worth anything

Chapter 8: The Coming of the Spirit

is the prayer that asks for our real desires. That kind of prayer is heard. That kind of prayer is answered. (From *The Secret of the Ages.)*

Mere lip prayers get you nowhere. It doesn't matter what your lips may say. The thing that counts is what your heart desires, what your mind images on your subconscious thought, and through it on Divine Mind.

Go where you can be alone, where you can concentrate your thoughts on your one innermost sincere desire, where you can impress that desire upon the Spirit within, and so reach the Father.

But even sincere desire is not enough by itself. There must be BELIEF, too. "What things soever ye desire, when ye pray, believe that ye *receive* them and ye shall *have* them." You must realize God's ability to give you every good thing. You must believe in His readiness to do it. Model your thoughts after the Psalmists of old. They first asked for that which they wanted, then killed all doubts and fears by affirming God's power and His willingness to grant their prayers.

What is it you want most right now? Ask yourself frankly—Is it good that I should receive this? Is it right? Will it work no injustice to anyone else? Then have no hesitancy in asking it of the Father—secure in the knowledge that anything of good He will gladly give to you. Here is His promise. Read it, and see if you can still doubt:

"I will say of the Lord, He is my refuge and my fortress: my God; in Him will I trust.

"Surely He shall deliver thee from the snare of the fowler, and from the noisome pestilence.

"He shall cover thee with His feathers, and under His wings shalt thou trust: His truth shall be thy shield and buckler.

Chapter 8: The Coming of the Spirit

"Thou shalt not be afraid for the terror by night; nor for the arrow that flieth by day.

"Nor for the pestilence that walketh in darkness; nor for the destruction that wasteth at noonday.

"A thousand shall fall at thy side, and ten thousand at thy right hand; but it shall not
come nigh thee.

"Because thou Hast made the Lord, which is my refuge, even the most High, thy habitation.

"There shall no evil befall thee, neither shall any plague come nigh thy dwelling.

"For He shall give His angels charge over thee, to keep thee in all thy ways.

"They shall bear thee up in their hands, lest thou dash thy foot against a stone.

"Thou shalt tread upon the lion and adder: the young lion and the dragon shalt thou
trample under foot.

"Because he hath set his love upon me, therefore will I deliver him: I will set him on high, because he hath known my name.

"He shall call upon me, and I will answer him: I will be with him in trouble; I will
deliver him, and honor him.

"With long life will I satisfy him, and show him my salvation."—PSALMS 91:6.

Chapter 8: The Coming of the Spirit

"Surely goodness and mercy shall follow me all the days of my life. And I will dwell in the house of the Lord forever." —PSALMS 23:6.

The Bible prepares us to do God's work, guiding us how to use our spiritual powers, offering detailed instructions to follow and practice.

Don't you suppose that you can follow them quite easily—can practice them successfully?

Let's try! In the volumes to come, I am going to do my humble best to continue to show the way.

WE HAVE BOOK RECOMMENDATIONS FOR YOU

The Power of Your Subconscious Mind by Joseph Murphy ABRIDGED - (Audio CD)

The Power of Your Subconscious Mind by Joseph Murphy MP3 [UNABRIDGED] (Audio CD)

Think and Grow Rich [MP3 AUDIO] [UNABRIDGED] by Napoleon Hill, Jason McCoy (Narrator) (Audio CD)

As a Man Thinketh [UNABRIDGED] by James Allen, Jason McCoy (Narrator) (Audio CD)

Your Invisible Power: How to Attain Your Desires by Letting Your Subconscious Mind Work for You [MP3 AUDIO] [UNABRIDGED] by Genevieve Behrend, Jason McCoy (Narrator) (Audio CD)

Thought Vibration or the Law of Attraction in the Thought World [MP3 AUDIO] [UNABRIDGED]
by William Walker Atkinson, Jason McCoy (Narrator)
(Audio CD)

CPSIA information can be obtained
at www.ICGtesting.com
Printed in the USA
BVHW032027091021
618612BV00001B/23